The Journey

A DAILY WALK WITH THE ROSE OF SHARON

RON AND PATRICIA OWENS

foreword by
TOM ELLIFF

A Word about the Cover:

The rose—most universally common and a beautiful flower.
Sharon—a large flower-covered fertile plain in the Holy Land, known
for its beauty and majesty.

JESUS, Rose of Sharon.

Published by Innovo Publishing, LLC
www.innovopublishing.com
1-888-546-2111

Providing Full-Service Publishing Services for Christian Authors, Artists & Ministries:
Books, eBooks, Audiobooks, Music & Film

THE JOURNEY
A Daily Walk with the Rose of Sharon

Library of Congress Control Number: 2018932676
ISBN: 978-1-61314-396-4

Cover Design & Interior Layout: Innovo Publishing, LLC

Printed in the United States of America
U.S. Printing History
First Edition: 2018

Contents

Foreword

W hen young Saul first set foot on the road toward Damascus, in a fit of over-zealous loyalty and ambition, little did he imagine that such a small step would thrust him out on a journey of epic proportion. This journey would involve an encounter with the living Christ, a radical redirection of faith, countless days of isolation and contemplation, challenges that would test the physical and emotional stamina of the best of men, and spiritual confrontations in arenas both great and small.

You are now familiar with the impact of that young man's life. As Paul, his journey would leave two-thirds of the Mediterranean world touched with the gospel of Christ in scarcely more than three decades. Finally, with trembling hand but unwavering heart, Paul would write from a Roman prison to his younger protégé, Timothy, about his journey's next and most significant step, urging him to hurry to Rome. "Come soon," Paul wrote, because "the time of my departure is at hand" (2 Timothy 4:6-8). Paul knew he was soon to set foot toward heaven.

Like Paul, your life is also a journey with Christ. Sometimes you find yourself on a mountaintop, inhaling the rarefied atmosphere of victory. At other times you are in the dark valley, needing light, direction, and encouragement. But most of the time, like Paul, you are plodding steadily onward and upward, enjoying intimacy with your Master, seeking spiritual stamina, and eager for the necessary rest that brings renewed strength for the journey.

This book is for you! Ron and Patricia Owens have brilliantly and touchingly captured the reality that life is, indeed, a journey. Long known for both lyrics, music, and a message that moves our hearts and stirs our spirits, the Owens have reached into the well of their own journey and now bring to us a refreshment that is, at once, both relevant and remarkable.

It has been my distinct privilege to share friendship with the Owens for over forty-five years. This friendship is of inestimable value to me, one I treasure, protect, nurture, and enjoy immensely. God has given the Owens the rare ability to speak into my heart at significant moments in my own journey with Christ. On more than one occasion, when needing to hear encouragement from the Lord, I have made it a point to find my way into a venue where the Owens were ministering, just to soak up the enduring but always freshly presented truth they were sharing. On some very special occasions, I've even been privileged to take the journey with them where I saw first hand their fervent spirits, raw but tender honesty, and eager quest for God's truth.

What you now hold in your hand is as much an *invitation* as it is an *instruction*. Through it, Ron and Patricia Owens are inviting you to join them on the journey. Just as you are encouraged by reading the journeys of the Apostle Paul, so you will be encouraged, inspired, challenged, comforted, and refreshed by the truth born out of the Owens' own journey with Jesus.

Rejoice evermore!

Tom Elliff,
2 Timothy 1:12

Pastor and President Emeritus
International Mission Board
Southern Baptist Convention

Introduction

While visiting with friends, a question was raised that really got our attention. Had we ever considered using our song poetry as a basis for a compilation of daily devotional readings? The question so surprised and impacted us that we felt we needed to take it seriously, though, over the years, others had told us how they used some of our songs for their personal quiet times. But to put together a series of readings using our song poetry as the scaffolding? We knew we had to take the matter before the Lord.

After a period of prayer and soul searching, we felt that this was something the Lord was initiating. So we began to work, looking to Him to lead us in selecting not just the song poetry but also the scriptures and circumstances that inspired their writing.

We began to realize that we didn't have to limit this compilation to just our own lyrics, so we have joyfully included some wonderful hymn texts written by others along with the background events in the lives of some of the authors that inspired them to write.

Some daily readings will contain complete stand-alone poems with scripture. Other entries will deal with a particular poem for more than one day because the different verses direct attention to particular truths that we feel need to be looked at more closely.

The process for this undertaking has been a spiritually renewing and challenging one for us. Who can adequately declare the excellencies of our glorious God and King? Yet, in spite of our limitations, we want with all our hearts to direct your attention to the One who has inspired all our music and poetry, and that of others.

> You are the song we sing, O Lord, fresh as the morning dew.
> A song of resurrection life, made possible by You.
> You are the song we sing, O Lord, You are our everything.
> Without You, Lord, we'd have no song,
> You are the song we sing! ✡

✡ = Poem by Ron Owens
+ = Poem by Patricia Owens

I

The Journey

I will instruct you and teach you in the way you should go. (Psalm 32:8)

Thomas said to Jesus "Lord, we do not know where you are going, and how can we know the way?" Jesus said to him, "I Am the way." (John 14:5-6)

Life is really but a journey made of days, weeks, months, and years.
Sometimes cloudy, sometimes cheery,
happy moments, sometimes tears.
But for those who trust in Jesus, it matters not what brings the day,
for He's promised to be with us as we walk along the way.

Like the travelers to Emmaus, so engrossed in how we feel;
thinking only of our problems,
we don't recognize the real
living Christ who's there beside us, every moment, every day.
Faithful Shepherd there to guide us as we walk along the way.

We are on a worship journey that begins with our "new birth."
It's a journey that continues
every day we're here on earth.
It's a journey that will climax when we enter heaven's gate,
there with every tongue and nation we will join in perfect praise.

When you think you've lost your bearing
and despair of getting home,
don't forget, with Christ beside you,
YOU WILL NEVER WALK ALONE. *

(Suggested reading: Luke 24:13-32)

2

This Is What I Ask

"Get in touch with your heart," the preacher said, "and present what you find there to God."

What does he mean? I thought. *How do I get in touch with my heart?* So I prayed, "Lord, what do you see in my heart?" And I went about the duties of the day.

The next morning, I found some old newspaper clippings. One of them included a photo of two family members that stirred some memories and feelings. All of a sudden, I realized the presence of resentment in my heart; one of the persons had caused much difficulty to the other, and it hurt me.

There it was! Resentment. God had shown me what was in my heart. I turned in confession to the Lord, asking for forgiveness and grace to release and forgive the offending person.

> This is what I ask, Lord,
> this is what I need.
> A fresh new look at You
> and an honest look at me.
> Though the looking shows me things
> I do not like to see,
> This is what I ask, Lord,
> this is what I need. ⁺

Search me, O God, and know my heart: try me, and know my thoughts:
And see if there be any wicked way in me, and lead me in the way everlasting.
(Psalm 139:23-24)

3

Each Step of the Way

The steps of a good man are ordained of the Lord, and he delights in his way.
(Psalm 37:23 KJV)

Our faithful God has promised He would lead
and guide us daily by His mighty hand.
He knows exactly what His children need
and works according to His perfect plan.
There have been mountains we've been asked to climb,
some rivers have been wide, some skies been grey.
The valleys have been deep and dark at times,
but without fail, our God has led the way.

We praise You, Lord, for all that You have done,
the lives You've saved, the victories You've won.
But You have said there's still so much to do,
the fields are white and laborers are few.
So Lord, we recommit ourselves to You today,
To follow You, our Master, all the way;
not quitting when we know what it may cost,
forsaking all for You, to gain the Cross.

Lord, You will lead each step of the way,
You will lead each step of the way.
So we'll praise You for the mountains, the valleys, rivers too,
for You never will forsake us,
Lord, You will always see us through.
You will lead each step of the way,
You will lead each step of the way.
We don't have to know the future, just trust You for today.
For You will lead every step of the way. *

4

Our God Provides

Seek first the kingdom of God and His righteousness, and all these things will be
added to you. (Matthew 6:33 ESV)

There is no need to look too far ahead,
for Jesus said to ask for daily bread.
We don't know what tomorrow has in store,
but that our God provides, we can be sure.

Provision that comes straight down from heaven above,
my needs provided by a God of love.
So for this day, and this alone I pray,
give me the strength I need, Lord, for today.

Lord, there are days when I don't understand
what You are doing, but I know Your hand
is wrapped 'round mine, and once again I see
You're all I need; You're my sufficiency.

Lord, make me neither rich, nor make me poor,
for in a rich estate, who can be sure
but that the riches take our minds off Thee,
or thankless hearts be born in poverty.

It's not for me to ask the *hows* or *whys*;
it is enough to know my God supplies.
I've tested this, and I know that it is true
that when I've trusted Him, He's seen me through. *

Look at the birds of the air, for they neither sow nor reap nor gather into barns:
yet your heavenly Father feeds them. Are you not of more value than they?
(Matthew 6:26 ESV)

5

The Greatness of God

High above on the throne was a figure like that of a man. I saw that from what appeared to be his waist up he looked like glowing metal, as if full of fire, and that from there down he looked like fire; and brilliant light surrounded him. Like the appearance of a rainbow in the clouds on a rainy day, so was the radiance around him. This was the appearance of the likeness of the glory of the Lord. When I saw it, I fell facedown. (Ezekiel 1:26b-28 NIV)

In a special treasured moment, the lyrics below were triggered as I stood mesmerized by the sight of a raindrop on a window pane. It was suddenly transformed into a prism by the early morning sunlight—producing all the colors of the rainbow. Afterward, as I opened my Bible, I found myself reading the verses above in Ezekiel 1, and my heart welled up in unspeakable worship.

> O the greatness of our God!
> Lord, I worship You; Lord, I worship You.
> You are holy, You're majestic in your glory,
> Lord, I worship You; Lord, I worship You!
>
> You are pure, perfect light,
> the colors of the rainbow shining bright!
> O the greatness of my God!
> Lord, I worship You; Lord I worship You! [+]

He wraps himself in light as with a garment. (Psalm 104:2 NIV)

6

Fullness

I pray that . . . you may be able to comprehend with all the saints what is the width and length and depth and height . . . that you may be filled with all the FULLNESS of God. (Ephesians 3:16-19)

I was sitting in a parking garage in Atlanta, Georgia, listening to a recording of Dr. Martyn Lloyd Jones interpreting the above scripture, when I heard him say, "One thing that the Lord requires is that we know our need of Him." Fortunately, I had a pad and pen with me. The following covers some of the points he addressed.

One thing that the Lord requires is that we know our need of Him. When we're hungry, when we're thirsty, when we see the awful sin that we're bent on turning after in our search for happiness, fullness, fullness, He has promised when we seek His righteousness.

Longing to be like the Master, He the object of our love. Longing for the heavenly manna that comes only from above. To be holy, just as holy as He says we're meant to be— less desire for self-fulfillment, more of true humility.

But to be more like the Master we must be the kind of clay that surrenders to the Potter as He shapes us day by day. Learning that it is in yielding to His will we find the key to the secret of His fullness: IT'S NOT I BUT CHRIST IN ME. *

7

Blessed Assurance

The Spirit bears witness with our spirit that we are children of God.
(Romans 8:16 ESV)

Phoebe Knapp, wife of Fairchild Knapp, founder of the Metropolitan Life Insurance Company, had already made a name for herself as a composer of music and verse when she visited her friend Fanny Crosby to share a new melody that she had just composed. After playing the music once on the piano, she turned around to find Fanny kneeling in prayer. Thinking perhaps Fanny had not been paying attention, she played it again. Fanny later wrote the following:

After my friend Phoebe Knapp had played the tune two or three times she asked me what the melody said. I immediately replied: "Blessed assurance, Jesus is mine. O what a foretaste of glory divine!" Within just a few minutes I had written verses and a chorus for my friend's new melody. First published in 1873, we sing it today exactly as the day the two friends wrote it.

Blessed assurance, Jesus is mine!
Oh, what a foretaste of glory divine!
Heir of salvation, purchase of God,
Born of His Spirit, washed in His blood.

Perfect submission, all is at rest,
I in my Savior am happy and blest,
Watching and waiting, looking above,
Filled with His goodness, lost in His love.

This is my story, this is my song,
Praising my Savior all the day long!

8

Fresh Springs

Whoever drinks the water I give him will never thirst . . . the water I give him will become in him a spring of water. (John 4:14 NIV)

It was a perfect setting for inspiration as I ran along the beach early that morning in Acapulco, Mexico. The sun, rising on the horizon, the waves, splashing on the shore, surrounded by the sight and sound of God's creation, I began singing, "You're the living water, springing up within. Flowing, daily flowing, cleansing me from sin. Check each thought and motive, wash away each stain. Cool fresh springs of mercy, make me whole again." Over and over I sang, "You're the living water springing up within." This would become the refrain to our song, "Fresh Springs," that Patricia would later set to music.

All my fresh springs are found in You, oh Lord;
all my fresh springs are found in You.
I long to drink from Your fresh springs, dear Lord,
springs that will cleanse me, and renew.
When I am weak, I find in them my strength,
You know just what I need each day.
Your Word's the food I really need to eat,
You quench my thirst along the way.

This world's become a barren place for me,
its springs no longer satisfy.
I once enjoyed to drink from them, you see,
but now its wells for me are dry.
Life-giving water comes from You, oh Lord,
Your springs abundantly supply
all that I need flows from Your springs, dear Lord,
fresh springs that never will run dry! *

9

The Process

We were teamed with Billy Strachan, principal of the Torchbearers Capernwray Bible School, founded by Major Ian Thomas. The occasion was a USAF/RAF retreat at the Hayes Conference Center in Swanwick, England. While there, Billy shared an illustration that became the inspiration for "The Process."

He told how one of their more successful Bible School graduates asked him one day why he had never been invited to speak at one of their Torchbearers conferences. Billy's response was simple: "You haven't been through the teabag process yet."

Without the boiling process, a teabag's of no use,
but when immersed its flavor is released.
And so it is with our lives, should God increase the heat,
our usefulness to Him will be increased.

The beauty of a diamond we know will not be seen
until some skillful cutting has been done.
An athlete knows that sacrifice and pain must be endured
before the victor's trophy can be won.

The breaking of its leg to help a lamb learn to obey
is sometimes what the shepherd has to do.
Without birth pains and labor, new life cannot be born,
nor until seeds will die can flowers bloom.

Lord, though I may not understand just what You have in mind,
I trust You for the grace to live this hour.
I trust that through the process the world I touch will know
the fragrance of Your beauty, love, and power. *

10

God Is Looking for a People

*I sought for a man among them who would make a wall, and stand in the gap
before me on behalf of the land, that I should not destroy it, but I found no one.
(Ezekiel 22:30 NIV)*

God is looking for a people who will crown Him as their Lord.
Who have turned from earthly pleasures, all the things this
world affords.
Whose allegiance is unquestioned, caring not what it may cost.
God is looking for a people who will glory in the Cross.

God is looking for a people who'll surrender Him their all;
with their eyes fixed on the Master, ready at a moment's call
to respond to His assignment, whether short, or whether long,
willing to change their agenda to the mission God is on.

God is looking for a people who'll spend time with Him in prayer,
those who've died to their ambitions, who will serve no matter where.
Those who're ready to surrender all they have, not just a part.
God is looking for a people who will give Him ALL their heart. *

Prayer

*Help me Lord, to be a person who surrenders You their all.
Who responds to your assignment, who will answer when You call.
Help me pledge You my allegiance, help me Lord to make You known.
May I truly be that person who is Yours and Yours alone.*

11

Peace, Real Peace

The faces across the table from us were not friendly. We were in the mayor's office in a strange new city in the former USSR. We had spent the previous thirty minutes listening, through an interpreter, to a monologue from the mayor about the virtues of communism and all the wonderful accomplishments of their country. He stared at us and demanded, "Do you think that your government really desires peace?"

Our response was, "Yes, we do think that our government really desires peace, but the only way any person can truly experience peace is through a relationship with Jesus, the Prince of Peace." He did not seem to like our response, so our interpreter quickly added, "They sing in Russian. Would you like to hear them sing?" Protocol seemed to require him to nod affirmatively. We then watched the change in his expression and eventually the unexpected tears in his eyes as we sang in Russian:

> Peace, real peace is found in Jesus,
> Peace, sweet peace down deep within.
> Peace, beyond our understanding,
> You can find real peace in Him.
> Hope, real hope is found in Jesus,
> Hope, sweet hope down deep within.
> Hope beyond our understanding,
> You can find real hope in Him. *

And this is still as true today for us all as it was when Jesus said, *"Peace I leave with you; my peace I give to you. It is not the kind the world gives . . ."* (John 14:27 NKJV).

I2

This Is the Truth

The Oxford Dictionary declared *post-truth* to be its 2016 international word of the year. Definition: "Objective facts are less influential in shaping opinions or beliefs," suggesting that the interpretation of actual facts is up for debate—that there is no longer such a thing as *absolute truth.*

But Jesus said, *"When He, the Spirit of truth comes, He will guide you into ALL truth"* (John 16:13 ESV). Jesus also said, *"I am the way, the TRUTH, and the life"* (John 14:6 ESV).

THIS IS THE TRUTH as we have received it,
these are the facts that are based on God's Word.
Christ died for sinners, and He was buried,
but on the third day He rose from the grave.
O hallelujah, Jesus is risen.
O hallelujah, Jesus is Lord!

THIS IS THE TRUTH as we have received it,
we all were part of the first Adam's tree.
But through Christ Jesus, the final Adam
we've now become part of God's family.
O hallelujah, Jesus, our brother.
O hallelujah, Jesus is Lord!

THIS IS THE TRUTH as we have received it,
we died with Christ on that old rugged cross.
But when He rose we rose with Him in victory;
now we are heirs and joint-heirs with our Lord.
O hallelujah, with Him we've risen.
O hallelujah, Jesus is Lord!

THIS IS THE TRUTH as we have received it,
when Christ ascended He promised to send
the Holy Spirit to comfort and guide us;
now He lives in us and we are His home.
O hallelujah, Jesus lives in us.
O hallelujah, Jesus is Lord!

THIS IS THE TRUTH as we have received it,
Jesus now sits at the Father's right hand.
There He is praying for every believer,
our Great High Priest, Intercessor, and Friend.
O hallelujah, Jesus is praying.
O hallelujah, Jesus is Lord!

THIS IS THE TRUTH as we have received it,
suddenly, Christ will appear in the sky.
Saints, dead and living, will rise up to meet Him,
at the last trump, in the blink of an eye.
O hallelujah, Jesus is coming.
O hallelujah, Jesus is Lord! *

13

This Is the Truth

(part two)

I delivered to you as of first importance what I also received, that Christ died for our sins according to the Scriptures, and that He was buried, and that He was raised on the third day according to the Scriptures. (I Corinthians 15:3-4 ESV)

THIS IS THE TRUTH as we have received it,
these are the facts that are based on God's Word.
Christ died for sinners, and He was buried,
but on the third day He rose from the grave.
O hallelujah, JESUS IS RISEN! O hallelujah, Jesus is Lord! *

"Facts that are based on God's Word." Oh, how important it is that we know these "facts" and that those "facts" are based on God's Word! We must begin with these foundational facts, which might be called the ABCs of the gospel: Christ died for our sins, He was buried, He was raised on the third day. He ascended back to His home in heaven as not only the Son of God, but now as the Son of Man!

The Apostle Paul considered these facts to be of first importance and went on to explain, *"if Christ has not been raised your faith is worthless: you are still in your sins. . . . But now Christ HAS been raised from the dead"* (I Corinthians 15:17, 20). Because He has been raised, our faith is not worthless.

CHRIST IS RISEN!
HE IS RISEN INDEED!

14

This Is the Truth
(part three)

And so it is written: "The first man Adam was made a living soul"; the last Adam was made a quickening spirit. Howbeit that was not first which is spiritual, but that which is natural; and afterward that which is spiritual. The first man is of the earth, earthy; the second man is the Lord from heaven. (I Corinthians 15:45-47 KJV)

THIS IS THE TRUTH as we have received it,
we all were part of the first Adam's tree.
But through Christ Jesus, the final Adam
we've now become part of God's family.
O hallelujah, JESUS OUR BROTHER! O hallelujah, Jesus is Lord! *

The "first" Adam (man) was of the earth, the "second" or final Adam (Christ Jesus), spiritual. The "first" man sinned, and that brought death into play, affecting all the human race. What a terrible, sobering condition we were in! But Jesus chose to put on human flesh, to step into our human condition, to become the second, the final "Adam." That changed everything!

For since by a man came death [first Adam], by a man [the final Adam, Jesus] also came the resurrection of the dead. For as in Adam all die, so also in Christ all shall be made alive. (I Corinthians 15:21-22)

Our heavenly Father sent Jesus to be our Redeemer.

He has delivered us from the domain of darkness and transferred us to the kingdom of his beloved Son, in whom we have redemption, the forgiveness of sins. (Colossians 1:13)

Jesus Our Brother!
JESUS IS LORD!

15

This Is the Truth

(part four)

What shall we say then? Shall we continue in sin that grace may abound? Certainly not! How shall we who died to sin live any longer in it? Or do you not know that as many of us as were baptized into Christ Jesus were baptized into His death? Therefore we were buried with Him through baptism into death, that just as Christ was raised from the dead by the glory of the Father, even so we also should walk in newness of life. (Romans 6:1-4 NKJV)

THIS IS THE TRUTH as we have received it,
we died with Christ on that old rugged cross.
But when He rose we rose with Him in victory;
now we are heirs and joint-heirs with our Lord.
O hallelujah, WITH HIM WE'VE RISEN!
O hallelujah, Jesus is Lord! *

Something mysteriously wonderful happened to us when Jesus died on the cross. Somehow, God included those who would trust in His Son in that awesome moment as He died the death we deserved, dying as our sin-bearer, paying the full penalty of our sins. But the wonder doesn't stop there, for He also included us in the victory Christ won as He triumphed over sin, Satan, and the grave. Jesus rose from the dead; He is our living Lord! We believe and trust in Him!

The Spirit Himself bears witness with our spirit that we are children of God, and if children, heirs also, and fellow-heirs with Christ. (Romans 8:16-17 NKJV)

WITH HIM WE'VE RISEN!
JESUS IS LORD!

16

This Is the Truth

(part five)

Jesus said: "Behold, I send the Promise of My Father upon you; but tarry in the city of Jerusalem until you are endued with power from on high." (Luke 24:49 NKJV)

THIS IS THE TRUTH as we have received it,
when Christ ascended He promised to send
the Holy Spirit to comfort and guide us;
now He lives in us and we are His home.
O hallelujah, JESUS LIVES IN US! O hallelujah, Jesus is Lord! *

A poignant moment is recorded for us in John 14. The Lord Jesus and the disciples were celebrating the Passover, and He told them that He would be going away and that they wouldn't be able to go with Him. They were greatly distressed by this news. In the context of all the amazing things Jesus shared with them during that meal, Jesus comforted them with these words, *"I will ask the Father, and He will give you another Counselor to be with you forever—the Spirit of truth. . . . you know him, for he lives with you and will be in you. I will not leave you as orphans; I will come to you"* (John 14:16-18 NKJV).

Notice that the promised Holy Spirit's coming to them was going to be just like Jesus coming to them: *"I will come to you."* What needed words of comfort to those bewildered and grieving disciples! Then, after the cross and resurrection, as He prepared to ascend to the Father, Jesus told them to expect not only a comforting Counselor but an empowering One who would live in them.

JESUS LIVES IN US!
JESUS IS LORD!

17

This Is the Truth

(part six)

And there were many priests, because they were prevented by death from continuing. But He, because He continues forever, has an unchangeable priesthood. Therefore He is also able to save to the uttermost those who come to God through Him, since He always lives to make intercession for them.
(Hebrews 7:23-25 NKJV)

THIS IS THE TRUTH as we have received it,
Jesus now sits at the Father's right hand.
There He is praying for every believer,
our Great High Priest, Intercessor, and Friend.
O hallelujah, JESUS IS PRAYING! O hallelujah, Jesus is Lord! *

After the Lord's Supper, as they headed toward the Mount of Olives where He would later be arrested, Jesus spoke some startling words to Simon Peter: *"Simon, Simon, Satan has asked to sift you as wheat. But I have prayed for you, Simon, that your faith may not fail"* (Luke 22: 31-32).

We can only guess how Peter may have felt at hearing those words, especially in the middle of such a challenging moment. But the need for us is to hear it in the context of our own lives. In the middle of our own challenging moments, whatever they may be—Jesus prays for me!

Who is the one who condemns? Christ Jesus is He who died, yes, rather who was raised, who is at the right hand of God who also intercedes for us.
(Romans 8:34 NKJV)

JESUS IS PRAYING!
JESUS IS LORD!

18

This Is the Truth

(part seven)

*For the Lord Himself will descend from heaven with a shout, with the voice of
an archangel, and with the trumpet of God. And the dead in Christ will rise first.
Then we who are alive and remain shall be caught up together with them in the
clouds to meet the Lord in the air. And thus we shall always be with the Lord.
(1 Thessalonians 4:16-17 NKJV)*

THIS IS THE TRUTH as we have received it,
suddenly, Christ will appear in the sky.
Saints, dead and living, will rise up to meet Him,
at the last trump, in the blink of an eye.
O hallelujah, JESUS IS COMING! O hallelujah, Jesus is Lord! *

This glorious truth of His Second Coming is the cherished,
strengthening promise that is given to all the redeemed of the Lord.
Included in this treasure is the promise that then we "shall always be with
the Lord!" What a hope and confidence we have!

As we wait for "that day," we want to take to heart this word of
admonishment for right now: *"And now, little children, abide in Him,
so that when He appears, we may have confidence and not shrink away
from Him in shame at His coming"* (1 John 2:28 NKJV). For He IS
coming—and saints, dead and living, will rise up to meet Him, at the last
trump, in the blink of an eye!

JESUS IS COMING!
JESUS IS LORD!

19

Rainbows in Stormy Places

George Matheson, the well-known blind preacher and hymn writer of Scotland, once wrote in his diary: "My God, I have never thanked Thee for my thorn. I have been looking forward to a world where I will get compensation for my cross, but I have never thought of my cross as itself a present glory. Teach me the glory of my cross. Teach me the value of my thorn. Show me that I have climbed to Thee by the path of pain. Show me that my tears have made my rainbow.

Thank You, Lord, for the rainbow, the promise of Your love and care.
Thank You for the sweet assurance that in the storm You're
  always there.
Thank You, Lord, for the rainbow that hovers over all my pain—
Thank You, Lord, for the reminder that there's no rainbow
  without rain.

Help me, Lord, to see Your rainbow, reflection of Your
  faithfulness.
Light that's shining in my darkness, the promise of Your peace
  and rest.
Thank You, Lord, for stormy weather that causes me to turn to You,
For the gentle rainbow's promise that You will always see me
  through.

Rainbows in stormy places, reflecting on the faces
of God's children who know He's always there.
Promise of His protection, child of the resurrection—
Sign of God's eternal love and care. *

20

Cruces Baratas
(Cheap Crosses)

If anyone desires to come after Me, let him deny himself, and take up his cross and follow Me. (Matthew 16:24 NKJV)

This cuts across the very grain of our humanity, yet it is fundamental to our being a true follower of the Lord Jesus. What does it mean to take up your cross? It obviously doesn't mean the health and wealth gospel that many western contemporary Christian leaders are preaching to multitudes who don't want to think of denying themselves anything.

A missionary acquaintance tells of an experience he had during a religious festival in Venezuela where he was serving. One of the festival's traditions was a parade in which everyone would carry and wave a handheld cross that could be purchased at a plethora of stores lining the parade route. Walking with the crowd, he suddenly noticed on a street corner a cart bearing a large sign: *CRUCES BARATAS EN VENTA* (Cheap Crosses for Sale). In other words, if you didn't want to put out much money for a cross, here is where you may purchase a cheap one.

One of the most poignant and challenging expressions about this matter of cross carrying is expressed in a hymn by Isaac Watts.

Am I a soldier of the cross, a follower of the Lamb?
And shall I fear to own His cause, or blush to speak His name?

Must I be carried to the skies on flowery beds of ease,
While others fight to win the prize and sail through bloody seas?

Sure I must fight if I would reign. Increase my courage, Lord.
I'll bear the toil, endure the pain, supported by Thy word.

35

21

Without

Now for a little while you may have to suffer grief in all kinds of trials. These have come so that your faith, of greater worth than gold which perishes, even though refined by fire, may result in praise, glory and honor when Jesus Christ is revealed.
(1 Peter 1:6-7 NIV)

Without the valley you can't have a mountain
Without the land there would not be a sea
Without the sun you cannot grow a flower
Without God's grace you cannot be set free

Without the clouds there would not be a rainfall
Without the rain you cannot grow a tree
Without the tree there would not be a forest
Without God's touch the blind would never see

Without God's joy you cannot cheer the weeping
Without His love you cannot warm the cold
Without His stripes no healing for the wounded
Without God's peace you cannot calm the soul

The love of God is greater than all hatred
The peace He gives will overcome all fear
His pardoning grace can cover every failure
His tender touch can dry up every tear

The love of God—beyond all understanding
It reaches even to our dark despair
Unending grace and everlasting mercy
A love with which there's nothing to compare *

22

Be Still, My Soul

We punched the replay button on the car CD player—again, then again, and again. We needed the words and music of the song to soak into our souls.

"In every change He faithful will remain." "Your God will undertake to guide the future as He has the past." "The waves and winds still know His voice who ruled them while He dwelt below."

Be still, my soul: the Lord is on your side;
Bear patiently the cross of grief or pain;
Leave to your God to order and provide;
In every change He faithful will remain.
Be still, my soul: your best, your heavenly Friend
Through thorny ways, leads to a joyful end.

Be still, my soul: your God will undertake
To guide the future as He has the past.
Your hope, your confidence let nothing shake;
All now mysterious shall be bright at last.
Be still, my soul: the waves and winds still know
His voice who ruled them while He dwelt below.

Prayer

Gracious Holy Spirit, thank You for bringing comforting, strengthening truth
to our hearts at just the "right" moment.

23

There Is Coming a Day

Behold, I tell you a mystery; we shall not all sleep, but we shall all be changed . . . in the twinkling of an eye. . . . the dead will be raised imperishable. O Death, where is your victory?" (I Corinthians 15:51-52, 55b)

There is coming a day, what a day that will be
when from earth's binding fetters at last I'll be free.
I will soar to my home in the sky where I'll meet
the One with the nail-scarred hands and feet.

By those scars I shall know Him, by the wounds in His side,
by the look of compassion and love in His eyes.
I shall bow down before Him, I will worship my Lord,
my Master, Redeemer, my Savior, my God.

There is coming a day, though I cannot say when
I'll be changed to the likeness of Jesus, and then
I will understand just what it meant when He died;
I will praise my Redeemer, when I cross the divide.

No more struggling with failure, no more crying or pain,
and to think I'll no longer be tempted again.
Oh, the joy just to know that one day I will fly
past the boundaries of earth to my home in the sky.

Hallelujah, O praise Him, O worship the King.
Let the heavens, the earth, let all nations now sing.
Glory, glory to Jesus, the Lamb that was slain—
Hallelujah, hallelujah, hallelujah, AMEN!
THERE IS COMING A DAY! *

24

My Prayer

The Lord is near to those who call on Him, to all who call on Him in truth.
(Psalm 145:18)

I need You, Lord, I seek You, Lord,
I want to meet with You.
O Holy One, God's only Son,
I set my hope on You!

Know my heart, and know my thoughts,
then by Your grace and power,
help me to trust and obey You, Lord,
and worship You this hour. [+]

Draw near to God, and He will draw near to you. (James 4:8)

Our need of Him is an ongoing condition, for we were not created to be self-sufficient. That need includes every aspect of life, even help in trusting and obeying Him.

Even for that need we look to Jesus, *"for we do not have a high priest who cannot sympathize with our weaknesses, but one who has been tempted in all things as we are, yet without sin. Let us, therefore draw near with confidence to the throne of grace that we may receive mercy and find grace to help in time of need"* (Hebrews 4:15-16).

25

My Father's World

The earth is the Lord's and the fullness thereof, the world and those who dwell therein. (Psalm 24:1 ESV)

The quiet beauty of a forest, the flowers awakened by the sun;
the majesty of snow-capped mountains,
the myriad colors of the dawn.
The twilight spell when day is ending,
the voice of nature joins in song;
do you know where this all began?
To whom does all of this belong?
THIS IS MY FATHER'S WORLD.

But midst the good of God's creation we see the evil caused by sin.
The threat of war and man's rebellion,
will peace and justice ever win?
We hear the wail of little children
who starve and very soon will die,
held in the loving arms of one
whose eyes have no more tears to cry.
IS THIS MY FATHER'S WORLD?

At times you feel like quitting, the work gets harder every day,
For greed and hatred keep prevailing
as man continues on his way.
Take hope, the story is not ended,
the final chapter's still to come,
lift up your eyes, pull back the veil,
God still is seated on His throne.
THIS IS MY FATHER'S WORLD. *

26

True Love

And now abide faith, hope, love, these three; but the greatest of these is love.
(1 Corinthians 13:13)

Jesus said: "A new command I give to you; love one another as I have loved you."
(John 13:34 NIV)

True love is patient and true love is kind
True love endures the tests of all time
True love's transparent, it walks in the light
True love's a candle that shines in the night

True love is hope when the going gets tough
True love's an anchor when seas become rough
True love is faithful through loss or in gain
True love's a comfort in suffering and pain

True love's a touch that speaks louder than words
True love's a whisper that barely is heard
True love's a hug that says, "I really care"
True love's a friend who will always be there

True love will share in your wildest of dreams
True love sees wonder in simplest of things
True love's a smile in a room full of frowns
True love lifts up when all else pulls you down

True love's a word that is gentle, yet firm
True love keeps giving when nothing's returned
True love's a hand when you're losing your way
True love still hears when you've no words to say

Continued on next page...

True love won't quit when the pathway gets steep
True love is strength in those times when you're weak
True love will guide but won't have to control
True love gives wind to the sails of your soul

True love may laugh at the oddest of times
True love gives meaning when nothing else rhymes
True love believes when all others despair
True love will carry what you cannot bear

True love's a shelter you find in the storm
True love's the fire that keeps a home warm
True love sheds tears, both of joy and of grief
True love is laughter when life needs relief

True love's a treasure that comes from above
TRUE LOVE'S FROM GOD BECAUSE
GOD IS TRUE LOVE *

27

May the Mind of Christ My Savior

Have this attitude [mind] in yourselves which was also in Christ Jesus . . .
(Philippians 2:5)

I watched her as she played the piano. I noted her wonderful musicianship and technique. But there was something else that especially got my attention—she was not just playing notes, she was playing the words of the song! It was obvious that those verses had special meaning to her, and she longed to convey them to those gathering.

Later, as we were together with her and her husband in a time of prayer regarding a situation where a Christ-like response was so needed, we heard her cry out, "Lord Jesus, press through, press through!" She wanted the nature and mind of Jesus to be expressed through her. She is with her Savior now. Her name: Heather Olford.

May the mind of Christ, my Savior, live in me from day to day,
by His love and power controlling all I do and say.
May the Word of God dwell richly in my heart from hour to hour,
so that all may see I triumph only through His power.

May the peace of God, my Father, rule my life in everything
that I may be calm to comfort sick and sorrowing.
May the love of Jesus fill me as the waters fill the sea;
Him exalting, self-abasing, this is victory.

May I run the race before me strong and brave to face the foe,
looking only unto Jesus as I onward go.
May His beauty rest upon me as I seek the lost to win
and may they forget the channel, seeing only Him.

28

Living Faith

Now faith is the substance of things hoped for, the evidence of things not seen.
(Hebrews 11:1 NKJV)

Faith is the substance of what you are looking for
before it has even arrived.
God says it, that settles it, so go act upon it
and you'll have a faith that's alive.
To get in on what God has promised His children
depends on some action from you.
As you dare to step out in faith you'll discover
what God says He'll do, He will do.

Living faith, trusting in the Lord.
Living faith, acting on God's Word.
Living faith in a promise that is true.
This is God's will, this is God's will.
This is God's will for you. *

*Faith enables the believing soul to treat the future as the
present and the invisible as visible. Faith is dependence
upon God, and this God-dependence only begins when
self-dependence ends. Genuine faith is more than mental
assent or an emotional experience. It is the inward
response to truth that has been revealed to the heart by
the Holy Spirit who quickens and makes our spirit alive.
(Manley Beasley)*

We are to walk by faith. We are to fight the good fight of faith.
We are to take the shield of faith. We are to ask in faith. We are sanctified
by faith. We are to draw near to God in assurance of faith.

29

Living Faith
(part two)

Without faith, it is impossible to please God. (Hebrews 11:6 NKJV)

*Faith is believing something is so, when it is not so, in order
for it to be so, because God says it is so. (Manley Beasley)*

It's not enough just to say you believe it
if you don't intend to obey.
God has so clearly revealed in His Word
how He wants us to live every day.
You'll find that you don't have to wait until heaven
to get in on what God has for you.
A faith that is living means more than just trusting,
it's doing what God says to do. *

If faith is just believing that God can do a particular thing, then
why is He not doing what we believe He can do? Could it be that our faith is
incomplete? If we expect God to be involved in or bless what we do, we must
operate by His rules. These rules begin by our finding out what is happening
in heaven—finding out what God has to say about it. *"Thy Kingdom come,
Thy will be done on earth as it is in heaven"* (Matthew 6:10).

We participate in bringing God's will from heaven to earth by
believing, trusting, obeying, and cooperating with Him.

Living faith, trusting in the Lord.
Living faith, acting on God's Word.
Living faith in a promise that is true.
This is God's will, this is God's will.
This is God's will for you.

30

Someday

For now we see in a mirror dimly, but then face to face. Now I know in part; then I shall know fully, even as I have been fully known. (I Corinthians 13:12)

I don't know why there is grief and pain, or why sorrow touches me.
I can't say why there is war and hate, or such bitterness and greed.
But I know that God loves me so, and His Word has promised me
that my strength will be as my days may be,
and His grace is my sufficiency.
So I'll wait, though my heart may ache, and I'll go on hopefully.
I'll trust in Him, wait for Him, and someday I shall see.

Someday I'll see the reason for it all,
someday all my heartaches and questions will seem so small.
Someday joy will break through sadness,
someday grief will turn to gladness,
someday when I see my Lord.
Till that someday, I'll trust Him with it all. ⁺

One aspect of that which we "now know in part" is expressed in I Peter 1:6-7: *"Now for a little while you may have had to suffer grief in all kinds of trials. These have come so that your faith—of greater worth than gold, which perishes even though refined by fire—may be proved genuine and may result in praise, glory and honor when Jesus Christ is revealed."* And the Apostle James adds, *"Blessed is the man who perseveres under trial because when he has stood the test, he will receive the crown of life that God has promised to those who love him"* (James 1:12).

31

It's All of Grace

Grace! 'Tis a charming sound, harmonious to the ear. Heaven with the echo shall resound, and all the earth shall hear. Saved by grace alone! (Philip Doddridge, 1755)

In Christ we have a righteousness
that God, Himself, approved.
Our Rock and our Foundation sure
that never can be moved.

By His own death our ransom's paid,
for this, His life was given.
God's law He perfectly obeyed,
through Him, we enter heaven.

When Adam sinned, he sinned alone,
yet in him all have died.
So by the righteousness of One
we all are justified.

It's by Christ's merit, His alone,
one day we'll take our place
among the blood-bought sons of God
we'll sing, "It's all of grace." *

*Amazing grace, how sweet the sound
that saved a wretch like me.
I once was lost but now am found,
was blind but now I see.*

32

Give and it shall be given to you; good measure, pressed down, shaken together and running over, will be poured into your lap. For with the measure you use, it will be measured to you. (Luke 6:38)

I gave away a smile today—it didn't cost a thing,
and though it only was a smile it helped somebody sing.
I could have kept it to myself as I have often done,
forgetting that such little things as smiles can help someone.

I gave away some time today to do a simple deed,
and though it really wasn't much it helped someone in need.
I could have used the time for me and failed to pass the test,
forgetting that it's as we give that we ourselves are blessed.

A smile, some time, a bit of care,
a little love left here and there,
a word of hope to calm a fear,
a tender touch, a listening ear,
in daylight, night, or early morn,
the love of Jesus is reborn. *

Prayer

*God spare me from self-centeredness,
help me to center in on You,
Save me from self-promotion too.
Teach me to seek another's good,
the needs of others help me see.
From selfishness, Lord, set me free.*

33

Any way, Anytime, Anywhere

Then I heard the voice of the Lord, saying, "Whom shall I send, and who will go for Us?" Then I said, "Here am I. Send me!" (Isaiah 6:8)

Any way, any way, here I am, Lord;
any way to bring honor to You.
I will go, I will stay, I am ready, Lord,
whatever You want me to do.

Anytime, anytime, here I am, Lord,
anytime of the night or the day.
Every moment I live is Yours, Lord,
anytime I will follow Your way.

Anywhere, anywhere, here I am, Lord,
anywhere—I surrender my all.
Here at home, overseas, anywhere, Lord,
I am ready to answer Your call.

READY TO ANSWER GOD'S CALL! *

Really? Any way? Going, staying, whatever He wants me to do? What if the assignment is not what I thought it would or should be? As one of God's children, we all have need of learning something the Apostle Paul said that he had to learn. He said, *"I have learned in whatever situation I am to be content"* (Philippians 4:11). Throughout our lives, we discover that God is a God of purpose, and He knows what He's about. He is able to cause His grace to abound to us and through us, whatever the assignment may be: any way, anytime, anywhere.

34

Any way, Anytime, Anywhere
(part two)

The following poem, written by a Welsh friend Elwyn Davies, then director of the Bible Christian Union, a mission outreach to Europe, was inspired by the words of Mrs. Hector MacMillan three months after her husband was martyred: "Young people," she said, "you may have to go farther than you think."

HOW FAR, LORD? How far?
Until the miles are meaningless and the well-loved scenes are lost;
till hearts are filled with weariness and men say, "Tis too great a cost."
How can I take the long road that leads o'er hill and dale
and drink the cup of loneliness right up to death's dark vale?
Is THIS what Thou dost ask of me? Is THIS my share of Calvary?
Until the miles are meaningless and the well-loved scenes are lost,
I'll walk with THEE, O Savior blest,
Till the last great range is crossed—
THAT FAR, LORD!

Any way, anytime, anywhere Lord;
serving You every day is my prayer.
Take me Lord, use me Lord, for Your glory,
ANY WAY, ANYTIME, ANYWHERE. *

35

Jesus, in Heaven, They're Worshipping You

Then I looked and heard the voice of many angels, numbering thousands upon thousands, and ten thousand times ten thousand. They encircled the throne and the living creatures and the elders. In a loud voice they were saying: "Worthy is the Lamb, who was slain, to receive power and wealth and wisdom and strength and honor and glory and praise!" (Revelation 5:11-12 NIV)

Jesus, in heaven, they're worshiping You,
bowing before Your throne.
Giving You honor, the honor that's due.
The worship that's Yours alone.
Lord, we now join with that music above,
adding our voice to their song,
singing: "Holy, majestic, infinite love,
to You all our praises belong." *

Praise the Lord from the heavens; praise Him in the heights! Praise Him, all His angels, praise Him all His hosts! (Psalm 148:1-2 NIV)

Praise to the Lord, the Almighty, the King of creation!
O my soul praise Him for He is your health and salvation.
All you who hear, now to His temple draw near;
Praise Him in glad adoration.

Praise to the Lord, O let all that is in me adore Him!
All that has life and breath, come now with praises before Him.
Let the Amen sound from His people again,
Gladly forever adore Him!

36

O Love that Will Not Let Me Go

Scottish minister George Matheson discovered that he was rapidly going blind while at Glasgow University where he had met and fallen in love with a fellow student. They were planning to get married, but when he broke the news of his impending blindness to her, to his astonishment and deep sadness, her blunt answer hit him with the force of a dagger to his heart: "I do not want to be the wife of a blind man," she said. And with that, they parted.

Years later, the memory of that rebuff came flooding back on the evening of his sister's wedding. He recalled the pain of that night that would trigger the writing of his most famous hymn.

O Love that will not let me go, I rest my weary soul in thee;
I give thee back the life I owe, that in thine ocean depths its flow
may richer, fuller be.

O Light that foll'west all my way, I yield my flick'ring torch to thee;
My heart restores its borrowed ray, that in thy sunshine's blaze its day
may brighter, fairer be.

O Joy that seekest me through pain, I cannot close my heart to thee;
I trace the rainbow through the rain, and feel the promise is not vain,
that morn shall tearless be.

O Cross that liftest up my head, I dare not ask to fly from thee;
I lay in dust life's glory dead, and from the ground there blossoms red life that
shall endless be.

37

Beauty for Ashes

The Spirit of the Sovereign Lord is on me. . . . to comfort all who mourn . . . to bestow on them a crown of beauty instead of ashes, the oil of gladness instead of mourning, and a garment of praise instead of a spirit of despair.
(Isaiah 61:1-3 NIV)

God never promised a garden of roses
without any hardship or pain.
God never promised a path without briars,
or a life of all sun and no rain.
No, but He's promised us strength for the journey,
and peace, knowing we are secure.
He's promised His presence right there in the fire,
His mercy and grace to endure.

Out of the wreck we rise to triumph,
out of the storms of life.
Out of the broken-hearted hour,
out of the pain and strife.
Beauty for ashes, God has promised,
hope, out of deep despair.
His inner peace when the lightning is flashing,
beauty, for God is there. *

God's presence with us means more than any of us can truly express. He is the reason it is possible for us to rise "out of the wreck" to triumph over despair and heartbreak. He is able to speak peace into our hearts. Beauty and hope are still real when God is there. *"Cast your burden upon the Lord and He WILL sustain you"* (Psalm 55:22 NIV).

38

The Quiet Time

Very early in the morning, while it was still dark, Jesus got up and left the house
and went off to a solitary place, where He prayed. (Mark 1:35 NIV)

THE QUIET TIME, THE QUIET TIME,
when I sit at Jesus' feet.
Those special, hallowed moments
when the earth and heaven meet.
Preparing for the day ahead,
I feast upon the Living Bread;
my soul's restored, my heart's renewed
IN THE QUIET TIME.

THE QUIET TIME, THE QUIET TIME,
the Savior's voice I hear,
communing with my blessed Lord,
His holy presence near.
I look into His matchless face,
I praise Him for His amazing grace,
I face the day, I go with Him,
FROM THE QUIET TIME. *

Prayer

Thank you, Lord, that as I go into my day I go
with the assurance that You go with me.

39

This Is the Sacrifice I Bring

I beseech you, therefore, brethren that you present your bodies a living sacrifice,
holy, acceptable to God, which is your reasonable service. (Romans 12:1 NKJV)

A broken heart, O Christ, my King; this is the sacrifice I bring.
And Lord, You never will despise a broken heart as my sacrifice.

My hours, my days, O Christ, my King; this is the sacrifice I bring.
And Lord, You never will despise my hours, my days, as my sacrifice.

My hopes, my dreams, O Christ, my King; this is the sacrifice I bring.
And Lord, You never will despise my hopes, my dreams, as my sacrifice.

My ministry, O Christ, my King; this is the sacrifice I bring.
And Lord, You never will despise my ministry as my sacrifice.

My life, my all, O Christ, my King; this is the sacrifice I bring.
And Lord, You never will despise my life, my all, as my sacrifice.

***

This place, O Lord, the altar, the offering, my life.
My body, Lord, I give to You, a living sacrifice.
Lord, I surrender all my rights, my will, my talents too.
Lord, not a thing would I hold back, I yield my all to You.
I yield my all, not just a part.
I yield my all, all of my heart. *

40

The Throne Is Occupied

Immediately I was in the Spirit; and behold, a throne set in heaven with someone sitting on it. And the One who sat there had the appearance of jasper and carnelian. (Revelation 4:2 NKJV)

You sit enthroned above the earth; You reign in majesty.
You'll judge with justice and in might throughout eternity.
THE CROSS IS BARE, THE TOMB IS EMPTY, THE THRONE IS OCCUPIED!

Just as Your name is praised above, may it be here below,
for who is like the Lord our God, from whom all blessings flow?
THE CROSS IS BARE, THE TOMB IS EMPTY, THE THRONE IS OCCUPIED!

Bow down, bow down before the throne; kneel in humility
before the One who rules and reigns in awesome majesty.
THE CROSS IS BARE, THE TOMB IS EMPTY, THE THRONE IS OCCUPIED!

Lift up your voices one and all to celebrate the King.
Shout loud, "Hosanna, praise to God," rejoice, rejoice, and sing.
THE CROSS IS BARE, THE TOMB IS EMPTY, THE THRONE IS OCCUPIED! *

Crown Him with many crowns, the Lamb upon His throne.
Hark, how the heavenly anthem drowns all music but its own.
Awake my soul and sing of Him who died for thee,
And hail Him as Thy matchless King throughout eternity.

The cross is bare!
The tomb is empty!
The throne is occupied!

41

The Lord Shall Choose for Me

Delight yourself in the Lord, and He will give you the desires of your heart.
(Psalm 37:4)

"Have you thought about marrying a second time?" he asked.

Oh, she thought. *Maybe he has found a special someone after the loss of his beloved wife.* The year was 1975. The one asking was a man her deceased husband had led to the Lord in Czechoslovakia many years earlier.

"Well," she replied, "I can see how you as a pastor really need a wife, but as for me, I haven't—"

"You don't understand. I'm asking if you will marry me," Vlado Fajfr interrupted. Such was the bombshell question with which Ruth Stewart was confronted. The reply came weeks later, after much soul searching and personal time with the Lord.

Years later, Ruth shared how the Lord helped her to deal with real issues. She said, "As an American woman, I had the desires of an American woman. If I wanted a blanket I could go to a store and buy one. A pair of shoes? I could go to a store and buy them. But if I moved to communist Czechoslovakia, that would not be possible. Then the Holy Spirit brought this prayer to my mind: 'Lord, plant Your desires in my heart. Cause me to want what *You* want; then, if I go to Czechoslovakia, I can have what I want.'" And that's what God did!

Day by day and with each passing moment,
strength I find to meet my trials here.
Trusting in my Father's wise bestowment,
I've no cause for worry or for fear.
He whose heart is kind beyond all measure
gives unto each day what He deems best.
Lovingly it's part of pain and pleasure,
mingling toil with peace and rest.

42

The Master Potter's Hand

Like clay in the hand of the potter, so are you in my hand, declares the Lord.
(Jeremiah 18:6)

By what I do, by what I think, by every word I say,
I'm fashioning my future, what I'll be like some day.
Brick on brick, stone on stone, little by little I grow
into the kind of vessel that eventually will show
if what I did, was what I wanted; following my own plan,
OR WHETHER I YIELDED TO THE MASTER POTTER'S HAND.

Yielded to the One who knows what's right;
following His leading, day and night,
even when I don't quite understand,
SUBMITTING TO THE MASTER POTTER'S HAND.

When the oven heat is turned up high,
I will sweat and strain, and sometimes cry,
and when broken, I will suffer pain,
But He who breaks always restores again.
Yes, He restores, but I won't be the same,
for thro' the breaking, thro' the melting, thro' the pain
I will be changed, I will be changed, and will more useful be
To my dear Lord, who lives in me. *

For me, to live is Christ ... (Philippians 1:21 NIV)

43

His Love in Me, Loving

Christ in you, the hope of glory. (Colossians 1:27b NKJV)

I have a choice, myself or Christ, each day I must decide
to go the way the world would lead, or in His will abide;
and as I seek to know His will, He makes it plain to see
that it is always best to let Him live His life through me.

His love in me, loving,
His mind in me, thinking,
His life in me, living, through the Spirit's power,
His eyes in me, seeing,
His heart in me, beating,
His voice through me, speaking, every waking hour. *

Frustrated, disheartened, bankrupt: there are days that begin like
that when we look at the challenges ahead and measure ourselves and our
resources to meet them. Too often we forget that we aren't left to cope
with the day in our own wisdom, strength, and personal resources. The
Lord Jesus not only chose to give Himself *for* us by His sin-atoning death
on the cross, but He has also chosen to give Himself *to* us—to live His
life through us.

> *It is encouraging to know that there is no demand made
> upon my life which is not a demand upon the life of
> Christ within me. (Alan Redpath)*

44

His Love in Me, Loving
(part two)

His love in me, loving,
His mind in me, thinking,
His life in me, living, through the Spirit's power,
His eyes in me, seeing,
His heart in me, beating,
His voice through me, speaking, every waking hour. *

His love in me, loving? What is "*His* love" like, especially in comparison to "my love"? To be honest, my love can be affected by the way I'm treated, by whether I get anything back when I give my love to someone. It can be affected by the way I feel on a particular day or by whether I get my way in a situation. Thank God the love of Jesus is not like that! When His love is expressed through me it will have these qualities:

> *Love is patient and kind; love does not envy or boast; it is not arrogant or rude. It does not insist on its own way; it is not irritable or resentful; it does not rejoice at wrong-doing, but rejoices with the truth. Love bears all things, believes all things, hopes all things, endures all things. Love never ends. (I Corinthians 13:4-8a ESV)*

What a difference there is when it is *His* love in me that is being expressed!

45

His Love in Me, Loving
(part three)

His love in me, loving,
HIS MIND IN ME, THINKING,
His life in me, living, through the Spirit's power,
His eyes in me, seeing,
His heart in me, beating,
His voice through me, speaking, every waking hour. *

His mind: My need is to have Christ's way of thinking operative in me. What *was* His way of thinking? What is something that can be observed and understood by what Jesus said and did when He lived among us? One obvious thing was His reliance upon His Father's guidance— He spent much time in prayer. He sought the Father's thoughts about everything, wanting to do His Father's will.

Jesus said, ". . . the Son can do nothing of his own accord, but only what he sees the Father doing. . . . I can do nothing on my own; . . . my judgment is just, because I seek not my own will but the will of him who sent me. (John 5:19, 30 ESV)

Wanting to know and to do God's will is a key expression of "His *mind* in me, thinking."

46

His Love in Me, Loving

(part four)

His love in me, loving,
His mind in me, thinking,
HIS LIFE IN ME, LIVING, THROUGH THE SPIRIT'S POWER,
His eyes in me, seeing,
His heart in me, beating,
His voice through me, speaking, every waking hour. *

I have been crucified with Christ, nevertheless I live, and yet not I, but Christ lives in me. (Galatians 2:20)

How can the life of Jesus be lived out through me? Here is where a wonderful truth concerning the oneness of the Godhead comes into play. Jesus told His disciples that when He would leave the physical world after His resurrection, He was going to send to them "another" like Himself. He promised that this "another" would be with them forever and would be *in* them. These two are so much "one" that in the coming of this "another," Jesus could say, "I will come to you" (John 14:16-18).

This One being sent to the disciples was the Holy Spirit. His presence in the hearts of believers is one of our identifying marks. *"If anyone does not have the Spirit of Christ, he does not belong to Christ . . . [but] if the Spirit of him who raised Jesus from the dead is living in you, he who raised Christ from the dead will also give life to your mortal bodies through his Spirit, who lives in you"* (Romans 8:9-11).

Precious truth! It is by the indwelling Holy Spirit's power that the *life* of Jesus can be expressed through me. His *love* in me, loving, His *mind* in me, thinking, His *life* in me, living . . .

47

His Love in Me, Loving

(part five)

His love in me, loving,
His mind in me, thinking,
His life in me, living, through the Spirit's power,
HIS EYES IN ME, SEEING,
His heart in me, beating,
His voice through me, speaking, every waking hour. *

There is an old saying in American culture that the eyes are the window of the soul. Though Jesus did not use those words, He did talk about eyes. He spoke of the eye as being "the lamp" of the body and being either "healthy" or "unhealthy." But Jesus was teaching about something more important than physical vision, and physical vision is not our consideration here. We are thinking about seeing people and situations in the way Jesus sees them: "His eyes in me, seeing," or we could also say, "looking through His eyes."

How did Jesus see the crowd that followed Him that day when He and His disciples were already so tired? They were trying to go to a desolate place by themselves to rest, but people from many towns ran and got there ahead of them. *"When he went ashore he saw a great crowd, and he had compassion on them, because they were like sheep without a shepherd"* (Mark 6:34 ESV). So he began to teach them and later fed them: five thousand men, and we assume additionally, women and children.

That is just one example of the great difference there is between "His eyes in me, seeing" and our human perspective being the lens through which we view other people and the situations we encounter each day. When we live, abiding in Him, His viewpoint will prevail in our lives.

His EYES in me, seeing . . .

48

His Love in Me, Loving
(part six)

His love in me, loving,
His mind in me, thinking,
His life in me, living, through the Spirit's power,
His eyes in me, seeing,
HIS HEART IN ME, BEATING,
His voice through me, speaking, every waking hour. *

"Above everything else," Solomon said to his son in Proverbs 4:23 (ESV), *"guard your heart, because it is the wellspring of life."*

Solomon is remembering what his own father, David, said to him when he was young: *"Lay hold of my words with all your heart. Keep my commands and you will live"* (Proverbs 4:4).

If our Lord's heart is going to beat in us, we're going to need to have a heart like David's who prayed: *"Teach me, O Lord, your ways that I may know your truth. Give me an undivided heart that I may fear your name"* (Psalm 86:11 NIV).

In Psalm 119:11 (KJV) he said, *"Your Word, O Lord, have I hid in my heart that I might not sin against you."* In Psalm 51:10 (KJV) he prayed, *"Create in me a clean heart, O God; and renew a right spirit within me."* No wonder David was considered by God to be a man after His own heart.

Your Word, O Lord, have I hid in my heart
that I might not sin against You.
Your Word, O Lord, is a lamp to my feet
and a light that will guide me through;
through all my days, wherever I go,
through all my life, I want You to know
Your Word, O Lord, have I hid in my heart
that I might not sin against You.

49

His Love in Me, Loving
(part seven)

His love in me, loving,
His mind in me, thinking,
His life in me, living, through the Spirit's power,
His eyes in me, seeing,
His heart in me, beating,
HIS VOICE THROUGH ME, SPEAKING, EVERY WAKING HOUR. *

There are numerous references in the Bible that address the voice or tongue issue. It was one of Solomon's concerns as he reminds us in Proverbs 10:19-20 that the person who holds his tongue is wise, and that the tongue of the righteous is like silver. Oh, to have a wise and silver tongue.

Most of us know how easy it is to make a verbal response to someone, or to some situation, that later we wish we could take back. And most of us have been on the receiving end of these kinds of remarks that have hurt. This kind of response is the antithesis of how Jesus responded to situations He encountered. Though He had hard words to say, especially to the religious leaders, what He spoke was either to correct, instruct, encourage, or comfort, but never to harm.

Is this not what the Apostle Paul is saying when he writes about *"speaking the truth in love that we may grow up in all things into Him who is the head—Christ"* (Ephesians 4:15 NKJV). At its core, this means that whatever we say, we are to say it in a spirit of love and caring. And we speak the truth in love when we care enough to speak the gospel into the lives of those around us, which is God's everyday calling for every Christian—speaking the TRUTH in love.

His VOICE through me, speaking, every waking hour.

50

Disruptions

Webster's dictionary defines disruption as "something that is thrown into confusion or disorder." Life is filled with interruptions, inconveniences, frustrations, and unexpected events. Things break, accidents happen. Traffic makes you late. Just when we don't need another added expense, an appliance breaks. Unexpected illnesses change carefully made plans.

Sometimes we handle interruptions to our plans poorly and react either in frustration or anger, forgetting that, though unexpected changes in our plans may catch us off guard, they never catch God off guard. A God-initiated change in plans is never a random, meaningless event. In fact, these interruptions are divinely placed in our path for a reason, and in our case, there was a disruption that would forever change the focus of our lives and would eventually lead us on a path that neither of us would have ever anticipated.

When we walk with the Lord in the light of His Word,
What a glory He sheds on our way!
For the favor He shows, and the joy He bestows,
Are with all who will trust and obey.

Not a burden we bear, not a sorrow we share,
But our toil He doth richly repay;
Not a grief or a loss, not a frown or a cross,
But is blessed if we trust and obey.

But we never can prove the delights of His love
Until all on the altar we lay;
What He says, we will do, where He sends we will go,
Never fear, only trust and obey.

51

His Eye Is on the Sparrow

Civillia Martin was a successful public school teacher in Nova Scotia, Canada, when she married American evangelist, William Martin, moved to New York State, and joined him in ministry. During their travels, Civillia met a woman in Elmyra, NY, who was an invalid. This led her to personally visit this lady in her home one day to encourage her. Civillia picks up the story.

During a time of conversation I chanced to ask her if she did not sometimes get discouraged? She answered: "Mrs. Martin, how can I be discouraged when my heavenly Father watches over each little sparrow and I know He loves and cares for me?" Procuring paper and pencil, in a few minutes I had written,

Why should I feel discouraged, why should the shadows come,
Why should my heart be lonely, and long for heaven and home,
When Jesus is my portion? My constant Friend is He:
His eye is on the sparrow, and I know He watches me.

"Let not your heart be troubled," His tender word I hear,
And resting on His goodness, I lose my doubts and fears;
Though by the path He leadeth, but one step I may see;
His eye is on the sparrow, and I know He watches me.

Whenever I am tempted, whenever clouds arise,
When songs give place to sighing, when hope within me dies,
I draw the closer to Him, from care He sets me free;
His eye is on the sparrow, and I know He watches me.

I sing because I'm happy, I sing because I'm free,
For His eye is on the sparrow, and I know He watches me!

52

Blow Like the Wind

I had awakened early for my usual morning run, and not knowing where else to go, I headed out on the highway in front of the motel where we were staying. Being quite early, I didn't anticipate much traffic. Wrong!

That morning, Mississippi's State Hwy 12 seemed to be the choice route of truckers. I remember almost being blown into the ditch a couple times by the swoosh of the wind as 18 wheelers flew by. How much that had to do with what led me to begin thinking about the wind of the Spirit, I don't know, but somewhere along Hwy 12, I began singing:

> Blow like the wind upon me.
> Burn like a fire within me.
> Flow like a river through me,
> Lord, with Your Spirit, refill me.

Subsequently, the remainder of the poem, set to music by Patricia, was written. We're reminded of what Jesus said to His disciples but a short time before He ascended into heaven:

> *I am going to send you what my Father has promised; but stay in Jerusalem until you have been clothed with power from on high. (Luke 24:49 NIV)*

Jesus said to His disciples it was best that He depart,
for then He'd send the Comforter to live within their hearts.
This promise was fulfilled the day the Holy Spirit came,
and the early church went forth in power, proclaiming Jesus' name.

Jesus said the Holy Spirit will not speak of Himself, but of Me,
He'll convict of sin, of righteousness and judgment yet to be.
He will lead you into truth, He'll exalt and magnify My name.
The years haven't changed His mission, His work is still the same.

...when He, the Spirit of truth, comes, He will guide you into all the truth; for He will not speak on His own initiative, but whatever He hears, He will speak; and He will disclose to you what is to come. (John 16:13 ESV)

Every day negotiations for world peace are made by men,
but Jesus said, to find real peace, you must be born again.
And in this birth the very nature of the Lord comes in,
and what takes place is not of us, this work is all of Him.

For we become containers for the life of our dear Lord;
we are His body, living stones, according to His Word.
And the power that raised our Lord from death,
that tore that veil in two, is available today to me,
He's available to you.

Blow like the wind upon me.
Burn like a fire within me.
Flow like a river through me.
Lord, by your Spirit, use me, use me. *

53

O to Be Like Thee

… whom he foreknew he also predestined to be conformed to the image of his Son.
(Romans 8:29a NKJV)

Born in a Kentucky log cabin in 1866, Thomas Chisholm would often say, "Aw, I'm just an old shoe." Self-educated, he began teaching in a rural school when he was sixteen and wrote this hymn-poem when he was twenty-seven. Just an old shoe? Little did he realize that the longing of his heart, as expressed in this hymn, would still be speaking to us today. Is this the prayer of my heart? Is this the prayer of your heart? God is at work in such hearts.

Oh! to be like Thee, blessed Redeemer,
This is my constant longing and prayer;
Gladly I'll forfeit all of earth's treasures,
Jesus, Thy perfect likeness to wear.

Oh! to be like Thee, full of compassion,
Loving, forgiving, tender and kind,
Helping the helpless, cheering the fainting,
Seeking the wand'ring sinner to find.

Oh! to be like Thee, while I am pleading,
Pour out Thy Spirit, fill with Thy love,
Make me a temple meet for Thy dwelling,
Fit me for life and Heaven above.

Oh! to be like Thee, oh! to be like Thee,
Blessed Redeemer, pure as Thou art;
Come in Thy sweetness, come in Thy fullness;
Stamp Thine own image deep on my heart.

54

Home

Home is a word that beautifully describes heaven—a place of *reunion* with loved ones who have preceded us "home." It is a place of rest from the power of sin—from the power of sorrow, suffering, and pain. It is a place of rest from the power of separation from those we love because there shall be no more death. It is a place of rewards and especially of the incomparable reward of hearing, *"Well done, good and faithful servant, enter into the joys of your Lord"* (Matthew 25:23 NKJV).

Face to face someday I'll see Him,
face to face beyond the sky.
Face to face I'll look on Jesus,
face to face, my Lord and I.

What a day, O what a meeting,
when I kneel before my King!
Tears of joy, my loved ones greeting,
crippled bodies now are leaping,
no more blinded eyes or weeping,
no more deafness, all can hear.
Tongues once bound join in the chorus
to the Lamb who stands before us.
Singing: *

> *Worthy is the Lamb who was slain, to receive power*
> *and wealth and strength, and honor and glory*
> *and blessing. (Revelation 5:12 NKJV)*

55

Rock of Ages

He was caught in a bad storm on a lonely moor in his native England. Pastor Augustus Toplady, acquainted with that area, quickly ran to take shelter in a nearby natural rock crevasse. The lightning flashed, the thunder rolled, and the rain descended in torrents, but Pastor Toplady was safe in the rock. As the storm raged, he thought of Isaiah 26:4 (KJV) that reads, *"Trust in the LORD forever, for in GOD the LORD, we have an everlasting Rock,"* or, as it reads in the margin of the King James version, "Rock of Ages." It was then that the first words of his familiar hymn began to etch themselves in his mind.

Rock of Ages, cleft for me, let me hide myself in Thee.

Returning home, continuing to be inspired by Isaiah 26:4, he finished what would become one of the best-known hymns of all ages.

Let the water and the blood, from Thy wounded side which flowed,
Be of sin the double cure, save from wrath and make me pure.

Not the labor of my hands can fulfill Thy law's demands;
Could my zeal no respite know, could my tears forever flow,
All for sin could not atone; Thou must save, and Thou alone.

Nothing in my hand I bring, simply to Thy cross I cling;
Naked, come to Thee for dress; helpless, look to Thee for grace;
Foul, I to the fountain fly; wash me, Savior, or I die.

While I draw this fleeting breath, when my eyes shall close in death,
When I rise to worlds unknown, and behold Thee on Thy throne,
Rock of Ages, cleft for me, let me hide myself in Thee.

56

The God of all Comfort

Blessed be the God and Father of our Lord Jesus Christ, the Father of mercies and God of all comfort, who comforts us in all our affliction so that we may be able to comfort those who are in any affliction with the comfort with which we ourselves are comforted by God. (2 Corinthians 1:3-4 NKJV)

It was a tough moment. I had driven my dear one to the airport and watched through the window of the concourse as he boarded the flight to begin the ministry journey that would take him overseas for three weeks. As I was still weak and feeling vulnerable after surgery and radiation, it was hard to see my husband leave. Fighting tears, I retraced my steps to the parking lot and got in the car to begin the drive back home. That's when it happened. Out of the blue, a line from a song I had not heard or thought of in many years came unexpectedly and clearly to my mind:

Safe am I in the hollow of His hand.

Where did that come from? Why did it come to my mind at that moment? I know without a doubt that it came from the Lord, and it came at that moment because He knew I needed to be reminded of His presence—He who is "the God of all comfort." Here is a hymn verse that reminds us of God's faithful presence in every situation.

In heav'nly love abiding no change my heart shall fear;
And safe is such confiding, for nothing changes here:
The storm may roar without me, my heart may low be laid;
But God is round about me, and can I be dismayed?

57

Forgiving, I'm Forgiven

Four months after her release from the Ravensbruck Concentration Camp in which her father and sister, Betsy, had died, Corrie ten Boom wrote a letter that pained her greatly. It was to the Dutch stranger who had betrayed her family for harboring Jews.

*The harm you planned was turned into good for me by
God. I came nearer to Him. I have prayed for you, that the
Lord may accept you if you will repent. I have forgiven
you everything. God will also forgive you everything if
you ask Him.*

God says if I would be forgiven, forgiveness I must show,
for as I'm willing to forgive, forgiveness I will know.

But Lord, the hurt, the pain, the scars, the memories of the past,
they rob me of Your healing power, they hold me in their grasp.

As long as there is bitterness I know I'll not be free
to love You as I ought to love and let You love through me.

Help me to die to anger, Lord, and to resentment too.
Help me to reach out now in faith and give it all to You.

Oh, how I need Your cleansing blood to sweep across my soul.
Lord, wash away my doubts and fears, and come and make me whole.

Amazing grace, how sweet the sound,
Christ died! Christ rose! Christ lives!
And by His resurrection power,
I CAN, I WILL, FORGIVE! *

58

Songs in the Darkest Night

Let him who walks in darkness and has no light trust in the name of the Lord and rely on his God. (Isaiah 50:10 NIV)

I'll sing a new song to replace my old song,
I'll sing a glad song to replace my sad song,
I'll sing a faith song, an amazing grace song,
for Jesus gives songs in the darkest night.
Yes, Jesus gives songs in the darkest night. [+]

It was one of those dark, rainy days, and there had been some initial talk of all flights being cancelled. Finally, we were allowed to board and had left the gate, only to be left sitting on the runway for more than half an hour as a storm cell rolled through.

The rain still falling heavily, it was at last our turn, and our pilot sent our large bird hurtling down the runway, lifting off skyward through massive dark clouds. And then, as we broke through, above those clouds, there it was: brilliant, beautiful sunlight!

The storm clouds had veiled the sun from our sight but had in no way affected its presence and power. The obvious application to life registered. The storm clouds in our lives may at times veil His presence from our anxious hearts, but the Lord Jesus is just as truly and reliably present as the sun was that dark morning, radiating His glorious love, faithfulness, and power.

59

His Name Is Jesus

*Therefore God also has highly exalted Him and given Him the name which
is above every name, that at the name of Jesus every knee should bow, of
those in heaven and those on earth, and those under the earth, and that every
tongue should confess that Jesus Christ is Lord, to the glory of God the Father.
(Philippians 2:9-11 NKJV)*

There are some who only know His name as just another name.
There are many who think there's no difference—that He's just the same
as all other prophets, sages, who've walked down through history,
that He died as any ordinary man upon that tree.
For they've never met my Jesus, they have never seen His face.
They know nothing of His boundless love nor of His saving grace.
They have never walked beneath the stream that flows from Calvary,
they know only what is said of Him, He's only history.

As for me, it has been different, for He gave me a new start.
I confessed my sin, believed in Him, and opened up my heart.
Then the saving, cleansing, healing blood He offered in my place,
erased my sins forever—oh, the wonder of that grace.
And I find in Him the power, overcoming power, to win,
in temptation's darkest hour, victory over every sin,
for He gave to me the right to use the name that set me free;
and before that blessed, holy name, the hosts of hell must flee.

His name is Jesus; yes, He's the One.
His name is Jesus, God's only Son.
His name is Jesus, bright morning star.
Come to this Jesus, just as you are. *

60

At the Name of Jesus

And God raised Him up to the heights of heaven and gave Him a name
that is above every name, that at the name of Jesus every knee shall bow and
every tongue confess that Jesus Christ is Lord, to the glory of God the Father.
(Philippians 2:9-11)

During times of suffering we can easily become self-centered, but forty-year-old Carolyn Noel, bedridden with a serious illness, rather than feeling sorry for herself, wrote the following words that lift our eyes away from self-pity to the One who deserves our worship and praise, no matter what the circumstances may be.

At the name of Jesus every knee shall bow,
every tongue confess him King of glory now;
'tis the Father's pleasure we should call him Lord,
who from the beginning was the mighty Word.

Humbled for a season, to receive a name
from the lips of sinners, unto whom he came;
faithfully he bore it spotless to the last,
brought it back victorious when from death he passed;

In your hearts enthrone him; there let him subdue
all that is not holy, all that is not true.
Look to him, your Savior, in temptations' hour;
let his will enfold you in its light and power.

Christians, this Lord Jesus shall return again,
with his Father's glory o'er the earth to reign;
for all wreaths of empire meet upon his brow,
and our hearts confess him King of glory now.

61

Worship

In John 12:1-8 we have the story of worship that takes place in the daily living of life. It's the story of Mary of Bethany who expressed her love for her Master in a very unusual but beautiful way.

Six days before the Passover, Jesus came to Bethany, where Lazarus was who had been dead, whom He had raised from the dead. There they made Him a supper; and Martha served, but Lazarus was one of those who sat at the table with Him. Then Mary took a pound of very costly oil of spikenard, anointed the feet of Jesus, and wiped His feet with her hair. (John 12:1-3 NKJV)

What Mary did revealed what was in her heart. True worship is the expression of our heart's devotion. Mary loved her Lord more than anything else. *The worship God is looking for begins with an "attitude of the heart" before it becomes an act.* And what Mary did revealed what was in her heart. May the words to this great old hymn express the attitude of heart I have for my Master.

My Jesus, I love Thee, I know Thou art mine.
For Thee all the follies of sin I resign.
My gracious Redeemer, my Savior art Thou.
If ever I loved Thee, my Jesus 'tis now.

I love Thee because Thou hast first loved me
And purchased my pardon on Calvary's tree.
I love Thee for wearing the thorns on Thy brow,
If ever I loved Thee, my Jesus 'tis now.

62

Worship
(part two)

Worship is the response of an adoring heart to the magnificence of God. In the truest sense of the word, it is the occupation of the created, us, with the Creator Himself.
(Ron Owens)

As Mary of Bethany watched her Lord and listened to what He was saying, she was so overwhelmed with love for her Master that she had to express her love outwardly. Her heart would let her do nothing less. She had to act on what was inside.

And so it was on March 2, 1791, as John Wesley lay dying, he surprised his friends who were gathered around his bedside by singing in a clear voice the following stanza of a hymn written by Isaac Watts.

I'll praise my Maker while I've breath;
and when my voice is lost in death,
praise shall employ my nobler powers.
My days of praise shall ne'er be past,
while life, and thought, and being last,
or immortality endures.

He could not hold it in! The next day he tried to sing that verse again but could only get as far as, "I'll praise . . ." Then, raising his hands toward heaven, he said, "Farewell, farewell. The best of all is God with us." With that he entered into the presence of his Lord, leaving behind him a well-worn clergyman's gown, a library of books, and the Methodist Church.

63

Worship
(part three)

Mary of Bethany was unashamed to let everyone in the house know how much she loved her Master. She knelt at His feet and wiped them with her hair. She was not embarrassed and risked ridicule and criticism, which she received from one of Jesus' disciples. But that didn't matter to Mary. Her favorite place was at the feet of her Lord. What a testimony for us. Is that where we'd prefer to be?

Billy Graham's soloist, George Beverly Shea, was given a poem at a very strategic point in his life. It was a poem written in 1888 by Oscar Bernadotte that expressed unashamed devotion and commitment to Jesus. The words so affected Beverly Shea that he tore up a contract to sing on a NYC secular radio station and set that poem to music, which he sang widely around the world for years to come.

> *I'd rather have Jesus than silver or gold,*
> *I'd rather be His than have riches untold;*
> *I'd rather have Jesus than houses or lands;*
> *I'd rather be led by His nail-pierced hand.*
>
> *I'd rather have Jesus than men's applause,*
> *I'd rather be faithful to His dear cause;*
> *I'd rather have Jesus than worldwide fame;*
> *I'd rather be true to His holy name,*
>
> *Than to be the king of a vast domain*
> *or be held in sin's dread sway.*
> *I'd rather have Jesus than anything*
> *this world affords today.*

64

Worship
(part four)

. . . And the house was filled with the fragrance of the perfume. (John 12:3b)

The worship that Mary of Bethany offered that day had an effect on her and on others. I call this the *aroma factor.* Though our motive in worshiping is not to get for ourselves but to give to God, we the worshipers are always the recipients of His blessing beyond anything that we could imagine. Mary carried the fragrance of her worship with her for days to come. It was on her hands, it was in her hair, it was everywhere she went: the aroma of a worshiper! She had made the sacrifice of worship, and she carried the result of that sacrifice with her.

But she was not the only one affected by what she had done. Everyone in the house that day was touched by the aroma of Mary's worship. The fragrance of her offering was an unmistakable testimony to her love for Jesus. In Ephesians 5:1-2 (NKJV) Paul admonishes the church at Ephesus to *"be followers of God as dear children. And walk in love, as Christ also has loved us and given Himself for us, an offering and a sacrifice to God for a sweet smelling aroma."*

Every true sacrifice, every true act of worship, rises not only to God as a sweet-smelling aroma, but the aroma of our worship affects others. The aroma, the witness of Mary's worship, is still affecting us today.

> May my life be a testimony to who I am in You,
> to who You are in me.
> Lord Jesus, may the ones I touch be touched by Thee.
> Oh, may my life be a testimony. *

The Journey

65

Ever, Only, All for Thee

She was the daughter of a pastor. She was converted at the age of fourteen, became ill at sixteen, and for the rest of her life was an invalid. She wrote that she was comforted to think that God was leading her to be a messenger to His children in distress.

In spite of her frail health, Frances Ridley Havergal became proficient in English, French, Italian, German, Latin, Greek, and Hebrew, and by the age of twenty-two, she had memorized the four Gospels, the Epistles, Revelation, Psalms, and Isaiah.

One evening, after experiencing a miraculous answer to prayer, Frances said, "I was too happy to sleep and passed the night in praise and renewal of my own consecration and these couplets formed themselves in my heart and eventually finished with, 'Ever, only, ALL for Thee.'" That night she wrote,

Take my life and let it be consecrated, Lord, to Thee.
Take my moments and my days, let them flow in endless praise.
Take my hands and let them move at the impulse of Thy love.
Take my feet and let them be swift and beautiful for Thee.

Take my voice and let me sing, always, only for my King.
Take my lips and let them be filled with messages from Thee.
Take my silver and my gold, not a mite would I withhold.
Take my intellect and use every power as Thou shalt choose.

Take my will and make it Thine, it shall be no longer mine.
Take my heart, it is Thine own, it shall be Thy royal throne.
Take my love, my Lord, I pour at Thy feet its treasure store.
Take myself and I will be EVER, ONLY, ALL FOR THEE.

82

66

The Stillness of a Silent Sound

The Lord is in His holy temple. Let all the earth keep silent before Him.
(Habakkuk 2:20)

It was a sacred moment as dear Stephen Olford led us into a time of corporate prayer. It was not the first time we had heard him use those words, helping us to "set the stage" in our own minds and hearts as we began to pray. These were words from an old hymn that had etched themselves into his heart as a younger man: "Speak, Lord, in the stillness, while I wait on Thee. Hushed my heart to listen in expectancy." The memory causes us to search our hearts anew. Is there enough silence in our lives?

Sometimes we think we're doing well,
but our heart may be full of sin;
and little will we know how much until we get alone with Him.
Until we're able to get past the noisy questions of the head,
until our "self," with all its pride, is laid before the Lord as dead.

How can we hear God's still small voice
with music blaring in our ears,
or know the peace the Spirit brings,
the touch that calms our inner fears?
Until we're willing to shut out the noisiness of life around,
willing to wait until we know the "stillness of a silent sound."

We are afraid to get too still, for in those quiet moments we
will have to face just what we are, something we may not like to see;
the attitudes that grieve our Lord, the pride,
the failures, how we've been;
but that is why we need so much those quiet times alone with Him. *

67

Try Praising the Lord

In everything give thanks for this is the will of God for you in Christ Jesus.
(1 Thessalonians 5:18)

I was carrying a heavy burden when I began that early morning run. We were facing a substantial financial crisis relating to our ministry property in Switzerland, and we knew it was going to take a miracle if we were going to meet a payment deadline.

Suddenly I heard a *swoosh*. I looked up to see, not just one, but two meteorites, then a third, shooting across the star-studded sky. I stopped to gaze at the heavens, and as I did, I became overwhelmed at the wonder of God's creation. I fell to my knees and began to weep. I don't know for how long, but I do remember that when I began to run again, the burden had lifted. I began praising the Lord at the top of my voice and soon found myself singing a new song.

Try praising the Lord. Try praising the Lord.
Try praising, try thanking, try praising the Lord.

On and on I ran—mile after mile. And yes, later that day—a miracle!

When you find that the valley is lonely and deep,
or the trails on the mountain keep getting more steep;
in those nights when it is harder to laugh than to weep,
have you thought about praising the Lord?

When the sandcastles built in the dreams you have dreamed
start to crumble and fall and all hope seems to end.
When you wish you could turn and start over again,
why not stop, and try praising the Lord? *

68

Grace

For by grace you have been saved, through faith, and that not of yourselves; it is the gift of God, not of works, lest anyone should boast. (Ephesians 2:8-9)

I once was dead, but by God's grace I have been made alive!
It is the mercy of my God, through Him I'm justified.
Just as if I had never sinned, complete in Christ I rest.
Assured of this, I now am clothed in His own righteousness.

In sin I came into this world, in helplessness was born.
Bound by the chains of Adam's race, in darkness I was formed,
without the strength to even cry, "Oh, God, help me to see."
Then, in regenerating power, God came, God came to me.

The myst'ry of redeeming love, I cannot understand.
Beyond all human means to know, the depth of God's own plan.
Giving to me the gift of faith so that I might believe.
Oh, hallelujah, praise His name, this gift I have received.

I'm saved, I'm saved, praise God, I now am saved;
Though worthy only of God's wrath, by grace I have been saved.
Not of my works, lest I should boast; nothing that I have done.
It's all God's mercy, all His love, it's by God's grace alone! *

69

Lord, Teach Us to Pray

And it came about that while He was praying in a certain place, after He had finished, one of His disciples said to Him, "Lord, teach us to pray..." (Luke 11:1)

Lord, teach us to pray, there's darkness all around us.
Teach us to pray, Your presence gives us light!
Teach us to pray, remembering Your promises.
Teach us, oh, teach us, Lord, to pray!

Lord, teach us to pray, though darkness be around us.
Teach us to pray, Your presence gives us light!
Teach us to pray, remembering Your faithfulness.
Teach us, oh, teach us, Lord, to pray! [+]

"Strategy?" two veteran missionaries replied. "Prayer is the strategy!"

A promise from God may very instructively be compared to a cheque payable to order. It is given to the believer with the view of bestowing upon him some good thing. ... He is to treat the promise as a reality, as a man treats a cheque. ... he must believingly present the promise to the Lord, as a man presents a cheque at the counter of the Bank. He must plead it by prayer.

70

Good and Gracious God

Oh, taste and see that the Lord is good. (Psalm 34:8)

Good and gracious God, accept the praise we bring.
We know that if the world is dark we still have cause to sing.
Our lives are in Your hand, in Christ we are secure.
We sing with confidence and know Your faithfulness is sure.

Maker of this world, we see Your might displayed:
the sun, the stars, the living things, all these Your hands have made.
In this the day we live, there's nothing we should fear,
the God who made the universe is still our strength and shield.

Good and gracious God, how wonderful to know
that even when life's sorrows come Your mercies overflow!
You help us when we fail, restore us when we fall,
Your love renews our courage, and You hear us when we call.

Good and gracious God, accept the thanks we bring.
We glory in the cross of Christ, our God and risen King!
In Him we place our trust, His name inspires our song.
The name of Jesus Christ the Lord, to Him all praise belongs! [+]

71

Good and Gracious God
(part two)

God reigns over the nations; God is seated on his holy throne. (Psalm 47:8 NIV)

Good and gracious God, accept the praise we bring.
We know that if the world is dark we still have cause to sing.
Our lives are in Your hand, in Christ we are secure.
We sing with confidence and know Your faithfulness is sure. [+]

The morning headlines were depressing. A sampling of stories being reported included, "Nuclear Option: North Korea Defector says strongman could attack US"; "Death toll in Colombia mudslide tops 230 as rescuers race to find survivors"; and "20 are hacked and beaten to death at Pakistani Shrine." Is it true that "if the world is dark we still have cause to sing"? What assurance is provided us to base this hope upon? The psalmist points us in the right direction as he admonishes in Psalm 34:8, *"Taste and see that the Lord is good; blessed is the one who takes refuge in him."* And again in Psalm 28:7, *"The Lord is my strength and my shield; my heart trusts in him, and I am helped. My heart leaps for joy and I will give thanks to him in song."* And yet again in Psalm 36:5 as he rejoices, saying, *"Your love, O Lord, reaches to the heavens, your faithfulness to the skies."*

To wrap it all up, the Apostle Paul provides this truth focus: *"Who shall separate us from the love of Christ? Shall trouble or hardship or persecution or famine or nakedness or danger or sword? . . . No, in all these things we are more than conquerors through him who loved us"* (Romans 8:35, 37 NIV). Yes, our lives are in His hand, and IN CHRIST WE ARE SECURE!

72

Good and Gracious God
(part three)

"Listen to me. . . . I am he; I am the first and I am the last, My own hand laid the foundations of the earth, and my right hand spread out the heavens; when I summon them, they all stand up together." (Isaiah 48:12-13 NIV)

Maker of this world, we see Your might displayed:
the sun, the stars, the living things, all these Your hands have made.
In this the day we live, there's nothing we should fear,
the God who made the universe is still our strength and shield. [+]

In "this the day we live," things occur that could cause us to become fearful: the rapid rate of change, the increase in violence, tension between nations, tense relationships in the home or workplace, health issues for ourselves or our loved ones, financial pressures, increasing hostility in our culture toward those who love the Lord. These are just a few things that could generate fear in our hearts. What we need and long for is stability, protection, and strength for the challenges we must face.

Hear the Word of the Lord: *"I the Lord do not change"* (Malachi 3:6). He IS the needed stability for *"this day in which we live."* He is also the secure shelter we can run to. *"You are my fortress, my refuge in times of trouble"* (Psalm 59:16). And He provides strength: *"Do not fear, for I am with you; . . . I will strengthen you, surely I will help you"* (Isaiah 41:10). He is indeed a GOOD AND GRACIOUS GOD!

73

Good and Gracious God
(part four)

In the day of my trouble I'll call to you for you will answer me. (Psalm 86:7 NIV)

Good and gracious God, how wonderful to know
that even when life's sorrows come Your mercies overflow!
You help us when we fail, restore us when we fall,
Your love renews our courage, and You hear us when we call. $^+$

"*God is our refuge and strength, a very present help in trouble*" (Psalm 46:1). I had blurted the words out, surprising myself and my dad as we sat together at the kitchen table. We were still in stunned disbelief and grief that Mother had died suddenly due to an aneurysm in her heart. The Holy Spirit knew that we needed to hear those words of comfort and assurance and had brought to my remembrance that first verse of Psalm 46. His mercies flowed into that moment of sorrow.

Then there are the memories of personal failure, things that dishonor and grieve the Lord. We know we don't deserve His pardon and favor. King David also knew what it was to grieve and offend the Lord. He poured out this praise concerning our gracious Lord: "*He has not dealt with us according to our sins, nor rewarded us according to our iniquities. For as high as the heavens are above the earth, so great is His loving kindness toward those who fear Him. As far as the east is from the west, so far has He removed our transgressions from us. Just as a father has compassion on his children, so the Lord has compassion on those who fear Him, for He Himself knows our frame, He is mindful that we are dust*" (Psalm 103:10-14).

HIS LOVE RENEWS OUR COURAGE,
AND HE HEARS US WHEN WE CALL.

74

Good and Gracious God
(part five)

For God was pleased to have all his fullness dwell in him [Jesus] and through him to reconcile to himself all things, whether things on earth or things in heaven, by making peace through his blood shed on the cross. (Colossians 1:19 NIV)

Good and gracious God, accept the thanks we bring.
We glory in the cross of Christ, our God and risen King!
In Him we place our trust, His name inspires our song.
The name of Jesus Christ the Lord, to Him all praise belongs! [+]

Indeed all praise does belong to the Lord Jesus. In his letter to the "saints in Christ Jesus at Philippi," the Apostle Paul spells out some of the reasons:

Your attitude should be the same as that of Christ Jesus: Who, being in very nature God, did not consider equality with God something to be grasped, but made himself nothing, taking the very nature of a servant, being made in human likeness. And being found in appearance as a man, he humbled himself and became obedient to death—even death on a cross! Therefore God exalted him to the highest place and gave him the name that is above every name, that at the name of Jesus every knee should bow, in heaven and on earth, and every tongue confess that Jesus Christ is Lord, to the glory of God the Father. (Philippians 2:5-11 NIV)

Let us give Him the praise and thanks that He deserves.

75

Again

Why are you downcast, O my soul? Why so disturbed within me? Put your hope in God, for I will yet praise him, my Savior and my God. (Psalm 42:5 NIV)

> The heart that once could sing
> will sing again.
> The bird with broken wing
> will fly again.
> God's grace to face the day,
> the will to walk life's way,
> the faith to simply pray—
> revived again.
>
> The sun that once did shine
> will shine again.
> Lost joy and peace of mind,
> renewed again.
> The calm within the storm,
> the love that once was warm,
> the trust that has been torn,
> restored again. *

There are moments that may come to the child of God that simply knock the breath out of us. Even some of the best-known saints have had those types of life experiences. Many bear testimony to this and identify with these words: *"I would have despaired unless I had believed that I would see the goodness of the Lord in the land of the living. Wait for the Lord; Be strong, and let your heart take courage; Yes, wait for the Lord"* (Psalm 27:13-14).

76

Unlimited

What is impossible with men, is possible with God. (Luke 18:27 NIV)

Do two plus two always make four?
No! With our Lord they can make more.
Five little loaves, two fish? You say:
"Five thousand can't be fed that way!"
Five thousand? You just lend an eye
and watch those two fish multiply!
Unlimited what God can do,
unlimited His work *through* you.

We all have heard the story told
of Job whose faith was tried as gold.
And though he lost all of his wealth,
his cattle, family and his health,
he knew God's way was always best,
he did not fail to pass the test.
Unlimited what God can do,
unlimited His work *for* you.

"Lazarus is dead! You've come too late.
We told you, Lord, you shouldn't wait.
Now there is nothing we can do,
and we had put our hope in you."
Then Jesus simply called his name,
and from the grave old Lazarus came.
Unlimited what God can do,
unlimited His work *in* you. *

77

Revive Your Church, O Lord

Revival is God's work in the lives of His people that transforms them into what they were created to be. It is the returning to spiritual vitality of someone who has become dormant, stale, and dry. (Author)

Revive Your church, O Lord, Your mighty arm make bear.
You're speaking all across our land; Lord, give us ears to hear.
Revive Your church, O Lord, disturb our sleep of death.
Awake the smoldering embers now by Your almighty breath.

Revive Your church, O Lord, grant us a thirst for You,
a hunger for the Bread of Life; O Lord, our hearts renew.
Revive Your church, O Lord, exalt Your precious name.
Refill us with Your Spirit now, and set our hearts aflame.

Revive Your church, O Lord, we have profaned Your name.
Our hearts have turned so far from You,
we've caused You grief and pain.
Revive Your church, O Lord, have mercy now we pray.
O God, we long, we long to see revival in our day.

Send the Refiner's fire,
come purge away our sin.
Help us, O God, return to You,
revive Your church again. *

78

Testimony

We all ... beholding as in a mirror the glory of the Lord are being transformed into the same image. (2 Corinthians 3:18 NKJV)

May my life be a testimony
to who I am in You, to who You are in me.
Lord Jesus, may the ones I touch be touched by Thee.
Oh, may my life be a testimony.

May my life be a tribute to Your name.
May I seek first Your smile, not man's applause or fame.
Lord Jesus, if it means for You I suffer pain,
may I not fail to be a tribute to Your name.

May my life be a symphony of praise,
a song of hope and joy that fills my nights and days.
Oh, grant that I might never cease to always raise
to You a joyful symphony of praise.

May my life be a mirror of Your grace,
reflecting love that goes beyond all time and space.
Lord Jesus, may men see not me but Your dear face.
Oh, may my life be a mirror of your grace.

May my life be a testimony
to who I am in You, to who You are in me.
Lord Jesus, may the ones I touch be touched by Thee.
Oh, may my life be a testimony. *

79

A Thousand Songs a Day

I will praise the name of God with a song, and will magnify Him with thanksgiving. This also shall please the Lord better than an ox or bull, which has horns and hooves. (Psalm 69:30-31 NKJV)

A thousand songs a day could not begin to say
the words of thanks and praise I owe You.
And yet, O Lord, I raise this thankful song of praise,
because my heart must say, I love You!
I love You, my Lord! I love You, my God!
And so, O Lord, I raise this thankful song of praise,
because my heart must say, I love You! +

Now here is a happy thing! I can do something that truly pleases the Lord; I can praise His name with a song and magnify Him with thanksgiving! My doing this can be more significant than selling something that costs lots of money and then giving that as an offering to Him. When we delight ourselves in the Lord, remembering His greatness and His goodness, true praise and thankfulness enter our hearts. God sees that, and when we express that praise and thanksgiving in song, we truly please Him.

O come, let us sing for joy to the Lord, let us shout joyfully to the rock of our salvation. Let us come before His presence with thanksgiving; Let us shout joyfully to Him with psalms. For the Lord is a great God, and a great King above all kings. (Psalm 95:1-3 NKJV)

80

Wonder

Stop and consider God's wonders . . . (Job 37:14 NIV)

Lord, help me not to take for granted all the things I should enjoy.
Sometimes I'd like to wish and once again become a little boy.
So many things were new, and every day became a new adventure.
I didn't know . . . I wanted so . . . I ran to see . . . I felt so free . . .
But now I'm bound, for I have found
there's nothing new,
what must I do
to rediscover wonder?

Help me find the wonder, help me see the beauty in a baby's eyes.
Help me find the wonder, help me feel the grandeur
of the starlit skies.
Help me find the wonder,
help me love so deeply that my heart's set free.
Help me find the wonder, help me be all you intended me to be.

Help me find the wonder,
help me dream again
and sing again
and laugh again
and play again
and shout so all the world can hear . . .
"I'm free—I'm free—I now can soar, they're not just dreams,
they're so much more!"
For what I was I'll be again.
I'll hope, I'll dream,
I'll pray, and then—
I'll wonder. *

81

Use Me

Just as a body, though one, has many parts, but all its many parts form one body, so it is with Christ. For we were all baptized by one Spirit so as to form one body. Even so the body is not made up of one part but of many. (I Corinthians 12:12-27)

Just as the body of Christ serves as our Lord's hands, feet, eyes, and voice, so do we function as individual members of the larger body.

Take these hands, may they serve You in all they do.
Take this voice, may it speak day and night for You.
Take these feet, may they walk only in Your ways.
Take my mind, eyes, and ears, use them for Your praise.

Lord, by Your Spirit use me,
may Your light shine through me.
Lord, with Your life refill me
so the world around will see
Your hands extended to them,
reaching for them,
You loving them though me.
And show them, Lord, You died to set them free. *

Then I heard the voice of the Lord saying, "Whom shall I send? And who will go for us?" And I said, "Here am I. Send me!" (Isaiah 6:8)

82

God

O Lord my God, you are very great, you are clothed in splendor and majesty.
(Psalm 104:1 ESV)

We were being driven in an old green van—the trip would take over an hour. Our driver knew no English, and we knew only a few words and short phrases in Russian, so conversation was not really possible. All of a sudden, the driver began singing a very familiar hymn tune—singing the words in his own language as we joined him, singing in English! We sang and sang, and after a few moments of silence, he began again the same precious hymn. Though we could not converse, we could sing together about the greatness of our God!

Have you thought about it lately, just how great God is?
He's in charge of all that's happening, the world is His.
Galaxies not yet discovered, universes not yet found—
all that is and ever shall be by His providence is crowned.

Have you thought about it lately, just how great God is?
All the stars, the earth, the oceans, they all are His.
Have you watched a smiling baby? Have you seen a colt at play?
Have your eyes beheld the beauty of your God today?

Greater than the rolling thunder, flashing lightning, raging sea,
more majestic than the mountains, tend'rer than a flower is He.
Hallowed moments in the quiet of an evening's setting sun
all portray with awesome wonder what our God has done!

Have YOU thought about it lately, just how great GOD is? *

83

A Sun Without a Sphere

Jesus led them up a high mountain. . . . There he was transfigured before them.
His face shone like the sun. (Mathew 17:1-2 NKJV)

Ten thousand times ten thousand stand
around your throne, Most High.
Ten thousand times ten thousand
sound Your praise! But who am I?

I sing because You are my sun,
Your light has shone on me.
I'll sing until this life is done,
to You all praises be.

Your brightness, Lord, each day appears
fresh as the morning dew.
It lifts our spirits, calms our fears;
we rest secure in You.

You are a sea without a shore,
a sun without a sphere.
Your time, oh Lord, is evermore,
Your place is everywhere. *

The unsearchable greatness of the Lord is still the happy meditation of the believer; *"for the Lord God is a SUN and shield; The Lord gives grace and glory; No good thing does He withhold from those who walk uprightly"* (Psalm 84:11 NKJV).

84

Just Take a Step

I will lead the blind in a way that they do not know; in paths that they have not known I will guide them. (Isaiah 42:16)

Just take a step, you're not alone,
and where you stand is not your home.
God will not fail to lead the way
with fire by night and cloud by day.
Just take a step.

Just take a step, go through the door.
You've never passed this way before?
The desert's wide, the water's deep—
God never fails to guard His sheep.
Just take a step.

Just take a step, He'll hold your hand;
there lies ahead the Promised Land.
The giants may stand strong and tall,
but in God's strength they all will fall.
Just take a step.

Let's take a step; we may get wet,
but God has never failed us yet.
The river's wide, the mountain's high?
Our every need He will supply.
JUST TAKE A STEP. *

"*We walk by faith, not by sight*" (2 Corinthians 5:7), and we do so with confidence in the One who identified Himself as "*the Good Shepherd. . . . [who] lays down His life for the sheep*" (John 10:11).

85

My Faith Has Found a Resting Place

Forever, O Lord, your word is firmly fixed in the heavens, your faithfulness endures to all generations. (Psalm 119:89-90 ESV)

Can there be a purpose in a crippling ailment? Eliza Hewitt may have asked this question when, after being a successful public school teacher in Philadelphia, her career screeched to a halt when she became bedridden for much of the remainder of her life with a painful spinal problem.

Lying there, she could have been bitter, but instead, she studied English literature and began to sing and write hymns that would become standards in English hymnody. Hymns such as "Sing the Wondrous Love of Jesus," "Sunshine in my Soul Today," "More About Jesus Would I Know," and the following that has been a favorite of many over the years:

My faith has found a resting place, not in device or creed;
I trust the ever-living One, His wounds for me shall plead.

Enough for me that Jesus saves, this ends my fear and doubt;
A sinful soul I came to Him, He'll never cast me out.

My heart is leaning on the Word, the living Word of God,
Salvation by my Savior's name, salvation through His blood.

My great physician heals the sick, the lost He came to save;
For me His precious blood He shed, for me His life He gave.

I need no other argument, I need no other plea,
It is enough that Jesus died, and that He died for me!

86

More Love to Thee

Why are you cast down, O my soul, and why are you in turmoil within me? Hope in God; for I shall again praise him, my salvation and my God. (Psalm 42:5 ESV)

One night, as grief-stricken parents returned from visiting the graves of their two young children, the mother's emotions reached the breaking point. In despair she cried to her husband, "Our home is broken up, our lives wrecked, our hopes shattered, our dreams dissolved." Her husband's wise response was, "But it is in times like these that God loves us all the more, just as we love our own children more when they are sick or in distress."

Elizabeth Prentiss immediately took her Bible and began reading. She then searched her hymnal for comfort and came to "Nearer My God to Thee." As she meditated on that hymn and on the words of her husband, she began composing the following hymn-poem:

> *More love to thee, O Christ, more love to thee!*
> *Hear thou the prayer I make on bended knee;*
> *This is my earnest plea, more love, O Christ, to thee,*
> *More love to thee, more love to thee.*

> *Once earthly joy I craved, sought peace and rest;*
> *Now thee alone I seek; give what is best:*
> *This all my prayer shall be, more love, O Christ, to thee,*
> *More love to thee, more love to thee.*

> *Then shall my latest breath whisper thy praise;*
> *This be the parting cry my heart shall raise,*
> *This still its prayer shall be, more love, O Christ, to thee,*
> *More love to thee, more love to thee.*

87

Forever Forgiven

He forgave us all our sin . . . he took it away, nailing it to the cross.
(Colossians 2:13-14 NIV)

The cross is that point in history
where eternity merges with time.
The guilt of a world meets the Savior;
the sins that He carried were mine.
Through the blood of my blessed Redeemer
I have been reinstated with Him,
the past is forgotten and buried
for God has forgiven my sin. *

Something cataclysmic occurred in history at the cross of Jesus Christ—eternity and time came into pulsating alignment. In the eternal purpose of God (Ephesians 3:11), it was the Lord Jesus who was hanging on that cross, not for any guilt of His own but for my sins and yours. *"He was wounded for our transgressions; he was crushed for our iniquities"* (Isaiah 53:5). Every one of us has rebelliously gone our own way, but *"the Lord has laid on him the iniquity of us all"* (Isaiah 53:6). The guilt of a world meets the Savior; the sins that He carried were mine—and yours.

Through Jesus' death something almost too wonderful to comprehend has taken place. It affects the standing before God of anyone who believes in Jesus. The Apostle Paul explains it: *"God shows his love for us in that while we were still sinners, Christ died for us. Since, therefore, we have now been justified by his blood, much more shall we be saved by him from the wrath of God. . . . We rejoice in God through our Lord Jesus Christ, through whom we have now received reconciliation"* (Romans 5:8-11).

Furthermore, God reassures us, saying, *"I am the One who wipes out your transgressions . . . and I will not remember your sins"* (Isaiah 1:43:25).

No longer can Satan accuse me,
when he does it is nothing but lies.
I tell him with each accusation,
"The blood of my Savior applies."
Not only for now, but forever,
I am sealed by the blood shed that day;
forever, forever, forever,
hallelujah, praise God, I can say:
"I'M FORGIVEN."

Satan, who is identified as *"the accuser of the brethren"* (Revelation 12:10), has no grounds to stand on as he spews out his charges against us. Our risen Lord Jesus is there in the courtroom of heaven, and the child of God will say, "The blood of my Savior applies; I'm FORGIVEN! Past, present, future, all my sins on Christ were laid. I've been adopted into God's own family; from the curse and power of sin I am set free. I AM FORGIVEN!"

88

Two Hills

We know love by this, that He laid down His life for us. (1 John 3:16)

On a Judean hill the sun shines.
The morning breaks so still, the sun shines.
Some people kneel to pray along the temple way,
while others stop to say,
"It's such a lovely day;
The sun shines."

But on another hill, the Son dies.
All heaven and earth stand still, the Son dies.
This is not just a day when children laugh and play
along the temple way where people stop to say:
"It's such a lovely day."
The Son dies!

This is man's darkest hour, when all of Satan's power
has rallied for the kill
upon a lonely hill.
The Son dies!
The Son dies!
GOD'S SON DIES!

Weep, yes weep, but don't despair,
for the reason He hangs there
is because He loves you, all because He loves you.

Greater love has no man known than the love of God's own Son.
Oh, how much He loves you! Jesus really loves you! *

89

Tetelestai
(Paid in Full)

The severed veil, His body slain, His blood upon the altar lain
has given us the right to come and kneel before the heavenly throne.
Christ entered that most holy place
and once for all the Savior placed
His own spilt blood and this sufficed,
there would be no more sacrifice.

We now can enter on our own; we can ourselves approach the throne
and kneel by His eternal grace and talk to God face to face.
Clothed in the righteousness of Him
whose blood has washed away our sin.
The earthly priesthood now has ceased,
and there remains but one High Priest. *

At the cross, as Jesus cried *"Tetelestai"* ("it is finished," or "paid in full"), at that moment, the veil in the temple was torn in two from top to bottom (Mathew 27:51). As He *"gave up His spirit,"* something momentous was taking place! Jesus was acting to overcome all that separates us from God's presence. His shed blood fully paid our debt. The resurrected Christ entered the most holy place *"through his own blood . . . having obtained eternal redemption"* (Hebrews 9:11-12). He, our Great High Priest, had made the perfect complete sacrifice. Because of that, we now have the privilege of personally approaching the throne of God (Hebrews 4:14-16).

It's finished, the debt's been paid,
the final payment has been made!

90

It's Friday,
but Sunday Is Coming

Looking down from the balcony of heaven, the angels watched as the body of Jesus was lowered from the cross. They saw Him wrapped in grave clothes, and they watched the small procession slowly make its way to the borrowed tomb. They heard the sobs of those who loved Him, of those He loved so much. They saw Joseph of Arimathea help place the body in His own tomb, and they watched as a large stone was rolled across the entrance. They saw Mary Magdalene and the other Mary sitting across from the tomb, weeping.

Hope was gone for the followers of Jesus.
They'd forgotten the things He had said.
Nothing left now but deep grief and questions.
No one thought He would rise from the dead.
They had helplessly watched their beloved
as He'd hung on the cross in such pain.
Though they wanted to, no one could help Him
as the crowd laughed and mocked Him to shame.

Satan tried at Christ's birth, through King Herod,
to destroy Him by royal decree.
He had worked every scheme he could think of;
now at last he would claim victory.
All the demons of hell were rejoicing,
they just knew that they'd finally won,
for they now had accomplished their mission,
they'd succeeded in killing God's Son.

It's Friday, but Sunday is coming. It's Friday, but don't you fear.
It's Friday, and the story's not ended, for on Friday, Sunday is near. *

91

It's Sunday!

Early Sunday, the Great God of heaven
looked down at the sealed garden tomb
where His Only Begotten lay buried,
bound by death's chains in darkness and gloom.
Don't despair, something's going to happen.
Don't give up, it's approaching the hour
when the Father will reach down from glory
and reveal His omnipotent power!

There's a flash, and an angel from heaven
blinds the men who stand guard at the door.
He rolls back that great tombstone in triumph,
for death's chains hold the Savior no more.

Where, oh grave, where, oh grave, is your victory?
Where, oh death, where, oh death, is your sting?
He, the Captive, has now become Captor,
Jesus Christ, Lord of Lords, King of Kings.

It's Sunday, our Savior is risen.
It's the Lord's Day, from death HE'S been freed.
It's Sunday, hallelujah, He's risen,
He is risen, He's risen indeed!

It's Sunday, our Savior is risen.
It's the Lord's Day, from death WE'VE been freed.
It's Sunday, hallelujah, He's risen,
HE IS RISEN, HE'S RISEN INDEED! *

92

What If?

What if Christ had not died?
Where would we be today?
No Easter morn to celebrate, but in its place just sin and hate,
unbridled lust, decay.

But come with me and see the place where Jesus lay.
It's not a myth, it's not a play,
from death to life He rose that day,
all doubting fades away.

Oh, hallelujah, glorious hour;
triumphant grace, redeeming power;
it happened as the prophets said,
MY JESUS CHRIST ROSE FROM THE DEAD! *

A 1946 film, "It's A Wonderful Life," presented a man of integrity who had given up personal dreams in order to help others. As George, facing financial ruin and arrest, attempts suicide on Christmas Eve, his "guardian angel" intervenes and shows the awful difference there would be in his community if he hadn't been there.

But here is the important question: *What if Christ had not died?* If He had not died and then been raised from the dead, there would be a truly awful difference in this world and in our personal lives. If Christ has not been raised, your faith is futile, and you are still in your sins. But Christ has been raised (I Corinthians 15:17-20). And He says, *"Fear not, I am the first and the last, and the living One. I died, and behold, I am alive forevermore, and I have the keys of Death and of Hades"* (Revelation 1:17-18 ESV). HALLELUJAH!

93

Touch Not the Glory

What do you have that you did not receive? If then you received it, why do you boast as if you did not receive it? (1 Corinthians 4:7 ESV)

During a "Women Alive" couples conference in Toronto, Canada, a lady, who looked to be in her midseventies, approached me at the end of one of the evening services and said, "This is for you," as she handed me a piece of paper. That was all. I didn't have time to engage her in conversation. I put the paper in my pocket, and when Patricia and I returned to our room later in the evening, I checked to see what had been given me. It was a handwritten poem, written by that lady whose name was signed at the bottom: Erma Davison. Subsequently set to music by Patricia, these challenging words have ministered profoundly to many through the years.

Should God call you to serve where others tried and failed,
But with God's help and strength your efforts will prevail
TOUCH NOT THE GLORY, for it belongs to God.

Have you some special gift, some riches you can share,
Or are you called of God to intercessory prayer?
TOUCH NOT THE GLORY, for it belongs to God.

Has God appointed you to some great noble cause,
Or put you where you hear the sound of men's applause,
TOUCH NOT THE GLORY, for it belongs to God.

A watching world still waits to see what can be done
Through one who touches not that which is God's alone.
TOUCH NOT THE GLORY, for it belongs to God.

94

And Can It Be?

"And Can It Be" was written by Charles Wesley immediately after his conversion on May 21, 1738. Wesley knew his Bible well prior to this time but had not yet experienced assurance of New Birth.

And can it be that I should gain an interest in the Savior's blood?
Died He for me, who caused His pain,
for me, who Him to death pursued?
Amazing love! How can it be,
that Thou, my God, would die for me?

He left His Father's home above, so free, so infinite His grace—
Emptied Himself of all but love,
and bled for Adam's helpless race:
'Tis mercy all, immense and free,
for O my God, it found out me!

Long my imprisoned spirit lay, fast bound in sin and nature's night;
Thine eye diffused a quickening ray—
I woke, the dungeon flamed with light;
My chains fell off, my heart was free,
I rose, went forth, and followed Thee.

No condemnation now I dread; Jesus, and all in Him, is mine;
Alive in Him, my living Head,
and clothed in righteousness divine,
Bold I approach the eternal throne,
and claim the crown, through Christ my own.

95

Almighty God

The heavens declare the glory of God, and the sky above proclaims his handiwork. (Psalm 19:1 ESV)

Almighty God, magnificent and holy!
Great is Your glory and awesome Your name!
You made the stars and set them in their courses,
Your works exalt You, Your deeds bring You fame.

Almighty God, we worship and adore You!
We join our praises with angels above,
through all our days our lips will tell the story:
Great is Your faithfulness, Great is Your love!

You are the Lord, let heaven exalt You!
You are our God, You're the Ancient of Days,
You are the Lord, and our hearts do adore You!
You are the Lord, and we bring You our praise. [+]

The Puritans used to say, "Think greatly of the greatness of God." A way for us to do this might be to stop and consider what He has created: the stars, for instance, and the sheer number of them! NASA states there are about two trillion galaxies, each containing between fifty and 250 billion stars—incredible! And although humans have named a few constellations of stars, there simply are many more stars than could ever be given names.

But . . . listen to what the Lord says: *"To whom then will you compare me . . . says the Holy One. Lift up your eyes on high and see: who created these? He who brings out their host by number, calling them all BY NAME"* (Isaiah 40:25-26 ESV, emphasis added). He not only created the stars and set them in their courses, He named them all! He *is* Almighty God!

96

Chosen

You are a chosen people, you are a royal priesthood, you are a people belonging to God, that you may proclaim the praises of Him who called you out of darkness into his glorious light. (I Peter 2:9 NIV)

We're chosen in Jesus, the Savior; chosen to praise His name.
Chosen to follow His footsteps, sometimes in suffering and pain.
He who identifies fully with every problem we face
promises strength in our weakness, and in each trial, His grace.

Daily He works to conform me, one day to be like His Son,
learning through hardship and trial, running the race I must run.
Pressured by life's circumstances, melted by heat of the fire.
Shaped in the hands of the Potter, climbing to plains that are higher.

Life still at times overwhelms me, driven by wind and by rain.
Crying, and feeling so broken, falling to rise again.
Stooping to sort through the rubble, my Savior's voice I can hear:
"I will give beauty for ashes; trust me, my child, never fear."

We're chosen, chosen in Jesus;
learning to be more like Him.
Chosen to follow His footsteps,
chosen to praise His name. *

Precious truth: God has chosen us! As Ephesians 1:4 tells us, *"He chose us in Him [Jesus Christ] before the foundation of the world, that we should be holy and blameless before Him."* He did this with love, purposing to adopt us into His family. As He shapes us to be like His Beloved Son, His compassions and love will never fail.

97

He's All I Need

A young pastor sat near the back of an auditorium in Chicago, waiting to hear Dwight L. Moody preach. He had come to the end of his rope and was planning to quit the ministry. During the early part of the service, the song leader made a statement that reached deeply into the discouraged heart of that young preacher: "Everything is in Jesus and Jesus is everything," Ira Sankey repeated. That was all A. B. Simpson needed to hear. Picking up his briefcase, he walked into a future that would profoundly impact his generation, including the founding of The Christian and Missionary Alliance denomination whose motto at one point became, "Everything is in Jesus and Jesus is everything! Go tell the world as fast as you can."

Jesus is all I need, He's everything,
He is the morning light, the song the robins sing.
He is the fire that warms the cold,
He is the greatest story ever told.
He is the shelter in the storm,
and He's the gentle voice of cheer to those who mourn.
He is the strong to all the weak,
He is the Shepherd who protects His sheep.

To hardened ground He is the plow,
and He's the healing touch upon the fevered brow.
He makes the bells of heaven ring,
He is the words and music angels sing.
To those who drown, a helping hand,
and for the lost at sea, to them He is the land.
He is the lighthouse on the shore,
and to the seeking heart, He is the door. *

98

God Loves Me

I pray that you . . . may grasp how wide and long and high and deep is the love of Christ, and to know this love that surpasses knowledge. (Ephesians 3:17-19 NIV)

God loves me, He loves me, His love is everywhere.
He is faithful, never changing, and He loves me.
I rest within His love and care! [+]

The ache of our human hearts is only answered when we *know* that God loves us. And yet, we realize that we don't deserve His love, so how could He possibly love us? The answer is found in who He is—*God IS love*—and in what He has done, *"God shows his love for us in that while we were still sinners, Christ died for us"* (Romans 5:8 NIV). It was when "we were still sinners," utterly incapable of earning His favor, that God chose to demonstrate His love for us. When the gracious Holy Spirit reminds us, and *"bears witness with our spirit that we are children of God"* (Romans 8:16), we learn to rest within His love and care. George Wade Robinson wrote verses that underline the wonder of coming to rest in God's love.

Loved with everlasting love, Led by grace that love to know,
Spirit, breathing from above, Thou hast taught me it is so.
O this full and perfect peace! O this transport all divine!
In a love which cannot cease, I am His and He is mine.

Heaven above is softer blue, earth around is sweeter green;
Something lives in every hue Christless eyes have never seen:
Birds with gladder songs o'erflow, flow'rs with deeper beauties shine,
Since I know, as now I know, I am His and He is mine.

99

Jesus, I Come

Thus says the One who is high and lifted up, who inhabits eternity, whose name is Holy: "I dwell in the high and holy place, and also with him who is of a contrite and lowly spirit, to revive the spirit of the lowly, and to revive the heart of the contrite. (Isaiah 57:15 ESV)

From barrenness to blessing,
from darkness into light.
From self-will to surrender,
from blindness into sight.
From brokenness to healing,
from stress and fear to peace.
From hopelessness to meaning,
from bondage to release,
JESUS, I COME.

Rebellion to repentance,
Your cleansing for my sin.
From bitterness to gratitude,
Your healing for my pain.
From my way, Lord, to Your way,
from judgment to Your grace.
From ashes to your beauty,
from doubting back to faith,
JESUS, I COME. *

Jesus said, *"Blessed are the poor in spirit, for theirs is the kingdom of heaven"* (Mathew 5:3 ESV). He does revive the spirit of the lowly and the heart of the contrite. Come to Him today.

100

I Believe

Abraham believed God, and it was counted to him as righteousness.
(Galatians 3:6 ESV)

I believe in God, the Three-in-One who made the heaven and earth.
I believe in Jesus Christ, God's only Son, of virgin birth.
I believe the Holy Spirit, love divine,
indwells and fills this heart of mine.
I believe, I believe.

I believe the Bible is God's Holy Word, of truth aflame.
He has blessed and magnified it as He has His holy name.
To redeem and save mankind the Savior died,
on Calvary's cross was crucified.
I believe. I believe.

I believe that someday through His boundless love and saving grace,
I shall rise on wings of light to realms above, I'll see His face.
There beyond the earth and air and sea and sky
I'll dwell with Him, no more to die.
AH THIS, PRAISE GOD,
I BELIEVE!

What is a belief? Many young children have a strong belief that the Tooth Fairy really exists. That kind of belief has little impact on life. The Bible speaks of an entirely different kind of belief. In Hebrews 11:6 we're told that *"he who comes to God must believe that He is, and He is a rewarder of those who seek Him."* This kind of believing involves entrusting ourselves to God—of taking into our hearts the things He has revealed in His Word, relying on those truths, relying upon *Him*. Who and what we believe really matters!

101

Your Word

Your word I have hidden in my heart that I might not sin against You.
(Psalm 119:11 NKJV)

How can I keep my living pure?
Oh Lord, how can I know for sure
that I am pleasing You today?
That I am walking in Your way?

Your answer's always been the same;
it's very clear, it doesn't change.
The answer is, "Your Holy Word,"
Lord, help me practice what I've heard.

It's IN Your Word that I will find
the thoughts with which to fill my mind.
It's THROUGH Your Word I'll know each day
how I'm to walk, what I'm to say.

It's WITH Your Word that I'm to stand
against the sin on every hand.
It's BY Your Word I find the power
to see me through temptation's hour.

I can be pure, I can be free
from sin's dominion over me.
But every day I've got to start
by hiding Truth deep in my heart. *

In His prayer for His disciples, Jesus elevated God's Word: *"Sanctify them by your truth. Your Word is truth"* (John 17:17 NKJV).

102

What a Christ Have I

Blessed be the God and Father of our Lord Jesus Christ, who has blessed us in Christ with every spiritual blessing in the heavenly places. (Ephesians 1:3 ESV)

I've found the Pearl of Greatest Price,
my heart now sings for joy.
And sing I must, for Christ I have;
oh, what a Christ have I.

My Christ, He is the Lord of Lords,
the Sovereign King of Kings.
The risen Son of Righteousness
with healing in His wings.

My Christ, He is the Tree of Life,
that will forever grow.
The living, clear as crystal stream;
eternal life that flows.

Christ is my meat, Christ is my drink,
my medicine, my health;
my portion, my inheritance,
Christ is my boundless wealth. *

An explosion of praise is only proper as we think about Him, our exalted Lord Jesus Christ! *"For from Him and through Him and to Him are all things. To Him be glory forever"* (Romans 11:36).

103

Lead Me in Your Way

O Lord, you have searched me and known me! You know when I sit down and when I rise up; you discern my thoughts from afar . . . and are acquainted with all my ways. (Psalm 139:1-3 ESV)

O God, you see my heart and know my actions.
You read each thought, there's nothing hidden from You.
There is no word I speak but that You hear it,
O God, you see, O Lord, you know.

And so, O Lord, please search my heart and motives,
look deep within and try my every thought.
Then in your grace help me to turn from evil,
and lead me in Your way.
That what I do and say
will show this very day
that I love You. [+]

Whoever has my commandments and keeps them, he it is who loves me. And he who loves me will be loved by my Father, and I will love him and manifest myself to him. (John 14:21 ESV)

104

Where Your Treasure Is

Where your treasure is, there will your heart be also. (Matthew 6:21 NKJV)

A rich young ruler came one day to Jesus,
to find eternal life, that was his goal.
When Jesus told him how, his heart was saddened,
for he loved his wealth more than he loved his soul.

What has become my motivating passion,
the most important thing to me today?
What are the goals right now I'm reaching after;
are they earthly treasures that will pass away?

One day when I have finished with life's journey,
and standing there before the Father's throne,
I'll give account of where I've stored my treasure,
will I hear Him say, "My faithful child, well done"?

Where my treasure is, it's very plain to see,
that's where my heart will be. *

What has become your motivating passion; what is my motivating passion? A speaker offered some diagnostic questions for his audience to help them find the answer. He asked, "Where do you spend your time? Where is your money spent? Where do your thoughts stray?" Jesus gave us this way to reveal the answer. He said, *"Where your treasure is, there will your heart be also"* (Matthew 6:21).

Prayer

Lord, help me to love You with all my heart, all my soul, and all my mind!

105

'Tis so Sweet to Trust in Jesus

You keep him in perfect peace whose mind is stayed on you, because he trusts in you.
(Isaiah 26:3 ESV)

The news on the pathology report that day was a blow. We were upset and fretful at the news because we didn't even understand what all the choices would be, much less which we should choose. But at that moment, God graciously brought His Word to our remembrance: *"In his heart man plans his course, but the Lord determines his steps,"* and *"The lot is cast into the lap, but its every decision is from the Lord"* (Proverbs 16:9, 33). His promise to be involved with us in the decision making brought peace. In that situation we were helped as we rested upon His promise, once again proving His faithfulness.

'Tis so sweet to trust in Jesus,
Just to take Him at His Word;
Just to rest upon His promise,
And to know, "Thus says the Lord!"

I'm so glad I learned to trust thee,
precious Jesus, Savior, Friend;
And I know that thou art with me,
wilt be with me to the end.

Jesus, Jesus, how I trust him!
How I've proved him o'er and o'er!
Jesus, Jesus, precious Jesus!
O for grace to trust him more!

These wonderful words were written by Louisa M. R. Stead in the late 1800s after a tragic event left her and her four-year-old daughter with no means of support except the Lord. Many years later, this hymn resonates in the hearts of present day Christ-followers as we have needs.

106

Brighter than the Morning

*He was transfigured before them; and His face shone like the sun, and His
garments became as white as light. (Matthew 17:2)*

You are brighter than the morning,
You're my Savior, You're my King.
Of Your beauty and Your glory,
Jesus, I delight to sing.
Never ending, never changing,
not confined by space or time,
clothed in light as with a garment,
crowned with majesty, divine. *

The extraordinary experience that the disciples—Peter, James,
and John—were allowed, seeing Jesus transfigured before them, was really
a sort of preview of the scene in Revelation 1. There the resurrected,
glorified Jesus is depicted as One whose *"eyes were like a flame of fire"*
and *"His face was like the sun shining in its strength."* This One identifies
Himself, saying, *"I am the first and the last, and the living One. I was
dead, and behold I am alive forevermore, and I have the keys of death and
of Hades"* (Revelation 1:14-18). Seeing Him with the eyes of faith, we
join with delight in singing, "Hallelujah, praise the Lamb!"

"Holy, Holy," cry the elders
as they bow, Lord, at Your feet.
And the angels join the worship
that one day will be complete
When the bride at last is gathered
from all ages, from all lands,
joining in that heavenly anthem,
"Hallelujah, praise the Lamb!"

107

Thank You, Lord

The mountains and the hills before you shall break forth into singing, and all the trees of the field shall clap their hands. (Isaiah 55:12 ESV)

Thank You, Lord, for Your beautiful things.
For ears that hear, for birds that sing,
for warmth of the sun on bubbling springs,
for eyes that can see Your beautiful things.

Thank You, Lord, for the flowers that grow,
for summer and rain, for winter and snow,
for mountains above and valleys below,
all speaking aloud of Your power and love.

Thank You, Lord, for the sorrows and sighs,
for winds that blow, for rivers that rise,
for rain that frames Your bow in the skies,
helping me lift my wondering eyes.

Thank You, Lord, for Your grace that has shown
the glory of God in the face of Your Son.
For Jesus who died, now risen above,
more glorious than all is JESUS—the gift of Your love. [+]

For God has shone in our heart to give the light of the knowledge of the glory of God in the face of Jesus Christ. (2 Corinthians 4:6)

108

If We Could See beyond Today

If we could see beyond today as God can see,
If all the clouds should roll away, the shadows flee;
O'er present griefs we would not fret
each sorrow we would soon forget,
For many joys are waiting yet,
for you and me.

If we could know beyond today as God doth know,
Why dearest treasures pass away, and tears must flow;
And why the darkness leads to light
Why dreary days will soon grow bright,
Some day life's wrong will be made right,
faith tells us so.

If we could see, if we could know, we often say.
But God in love a veil doth throw across our way.
We cannot see what lies before,
And so we cling to Him the more
He leads us till this life is o'er,
TRUST AND OBEY.

Sometimes we fret because we can't see beyond today. Jesus said, *"Do not be anxious for tomorrow; for tomorrow will care for itself. Each day has enough trouble of its own"* (Mathew 6:34). Our Lord knows what is best for us. When the Lord Jesus was preparing His disciples for the time that He would leave them, He demonstrated His tender care for them by saying, *"I have many more things to say to you, but you cannot bear them now"* (John 16:12). He knows when and what we can bear, and He shields us with His wisdom and love.

109

According to Your Faith

Jesus said to him, "What do you want me to do for you?" The blind man said, "Rabbi, let me recover my sight." Jesus said to him, "Go your way; your faith has made you well." (Mark 10:51-52 ESV)

One day along a country road a man walked slowly on.
No clouds in sight, the day was hot, the sun was beating down.
Around him walked a dozen men, they too were hot and dry,
when all at once the silence broke; they heard a blind man cry.

"Good Master, would you touch my eyes? Have mercy, Lord, on me."
And then were heard those words of hope that make the blind to see

"According to your faith, so be it unto you.
Be whole, my child; trust Me and you will see.
According to your faith, so be it unto you.
Ask, and you will receive—believe in me."

Today, our Lord's enthroned in heaven, He sits at God's right hand.
He knows exactly how we feel, He knows and understands.
And just the same as years ago, a pleading voice is heard;
and now, as He has always done, He listens to each word.

"Good Master, would you touch my eyes,
these eyes made blind by sin?"
And even now are heard those words that draw men unto Him.

"According to your faith, so be it unto you.
Be whole, my child; trust Me and you will see.
According to your faith, so be it unto you.
Ask, and you shall receive—believe in me." *

110

Even So, Come Quickly, Lord Jesus

Our struggle is not against flesh and blood, but against the rulers, the powers, the world forces of this darkness, against the spiritual forces of wickedness in the heavenly places. (Ephesians 6:12)

We don't have to look far to discover
that the world we have known won't last long.
Governments, and the folk who support them,
can't decide what is right or what's wrong.
Men who yesterday said they were certain,
say today that things aren't quite so clear.
Every day the world's news is confirming
that the Lord's coming back must be near.

What a day that will be when we meet Him,
when the church is caught up in the air;
when the trumpet announces that meeting,
we'll look up and our Lord will be there.
Many signs point to His soon appearing,
prophecies are fulfilled every day.
By the way things now seem to be going
surely Jesus must be on His way.

Even so, come quickly, Lord Jesus,
even so, fulfill Your Word.
Even so, come take Your bride away,
even so, come quickly, my Lord. *

The Lord Himself will descend from heaven with a shout . . . we shall be caught up to meet the Lord in the air. (1 Thessalonians 4:16-17 ESV)

III

Creation, Sing!

Let the heavens rejoice, let the earth be glad, let the sea resound, and all that is in it. Let the fields be jubilant, and everything in them; let all the trees of the forest sing for joy. Let all creation rejoice before the Lord. (Psalm 96:11-13a NKJV)

Sing to the Lord, creation, sing,
for He is worthy of praise.
Shout forth the glory of our King
and loud His anthems raise.

The dawn and sunset shout for joy,
He waters the earth with rain.
The rivers of God will not dry up,
His fields are covered with grain.

How awe inspiring are Your deeds,
how great Your might and power.
Yet in Your hand, how tenderly
You hold each bird and flower.

What confidence in trusting You,
Who cannot tell a lie.
What hope in knowing that one day
we'll meet You in the sky.

Sing to the Lord, creation, sing,
for He is worthy of praise.
Shout forth the glory of our King,
and loud His anthems raise. *

112

My Prayer

The Lord is near to those who call on Him, to all who call on Him in truth.
(Psalm 145:18)

I need You, Lord, I seek You, Lord,
I want to meet with You.
O Holy One, God's only Son,
I set my hope on You!

Know my heart, and know my thoughts,
then by Your grace and power,
help me to trust and obey You, Lord,
and worship You this hour. [+]

Draw near to God, and He will draw near to you. (James 4:8)

Our need of Him is an ongoing condition, for we were not created to be self-sufficient. That need includes every aspect of life, even help in trusting and obeying Him.

Even for that need we can look to Jesus, *"for we do not have a high priest who cannot sympathize with our weaknesses, but one who has been tempted in all things as we are, yet without sin. Let us therefore draw near with confidence to the throne of grace that we may receive mercy and find grace to help in time of need"* (Hebrews 4:15-16).

113

He Gives Us More Grace

He said to me, "My grace is sufficient for you, for my power is made perfect in weakness." (2 Corinthians 12:9 ESV)

After receiving the devastating verdict from her doctors that she would be a helpless arthritic invalid for the rest of her life, Annie Johnson Flint pushed a pen through her bent and swollen fingers and began to write, without any thought that it might one day be an avenue of ministry. What she wrote provided her solace in the long hours of suffering. But God had His plan in mind as Annie began making hand-lettered cards and gift books, decorating them with her own poetry, such as the hymn-poem below.

He gives us more grace when the burdens grow greater,
He sends us more strength when the labors increase;
To added afflictions He adds His mercy,
To multiplied trials, His multiplied peace.

When we have exhausted our store of endurance,
When our strength has failed ere the day is half done,
When we reach the end of our hoarded resources
Our Father's full giving is only begun.

His love has no limits, His grace has no measure,
His power has no boundary known unto men;
For out of His infinite riches in Jesus
He gives, and He gives, and He gives again!

***

In all this you greatly rejoice, though now for a little while you may have had to suffer grief in all kinds of trials. (1 Peter 1:6 NIV)

114

The Solid Rock

Upon this rock I will build My church, and the gates of hell shall not prevail against it. (Matthew 16:18 ESV)

From a London pub, to the city streets as an urchin, to salvation, to cabinet-making, to pastoring, to hymn-writing. Speaking about those early days, Edward Mote says, "So ignorant was I that I did not know that there was a God." He sums it all up in the following testimony.

*My hope is built on nothing less
than Jesus' blood and righteousness;
I dare not trust the sweetest frame,
but wholly lean on Jesus' name.*

*When darkness veils His lovely face,
I rest on His unchanging grace;
In every high and stormy gale
my anchor holds within the veil.*

*His oath, His covenant, and blood
support me in the whelming flood;
When every earthly prop gives way,
He then is all my Hope and Stay.*

*When He shall come with trumpet sound,
Oh, may I then in Him be found,
Clothed in His righteousness alone,
Faultless to stand before the throne!*

*ON CHRIST THE SOLID ROCK I STAND,
ALL OTHER GROUND IS SINKING SAND.*

115

Trust in Me

He was a man of sorrows, and acquainted with grief. (Isaiah 53:3)

It is all right to cry, my child,
I too have wept, You know.
And it's not wrong to wonder why
things go the way they go.
Just don't forget, I'll give you strength
to meet each trial you face;
remember always what I've said:
"Sufficient is my grace."

Your every thought is known to me,
I watch the things you do;
and every moment I'm in charge
of all concerning you.
There's not a thing that I'll allow
to cause you hurt or pain
that cannot turn out best for you,
earth's loss will be your gain.

TRUST in ME and you will see
my way is always best.
TRUST in ME and I will lead you, child,
into my rest.
I've promised that, as go your days,
for you my strength shall be,
I know it's hard, but you must learn
each day to TRUST in ME. *

A bruised reed He will not break. (Isaiah 42:3)

116

The Way that God Leads

You shall remember all the way which the Lord your God has led you in the wilderness . . . (Deuteronomy 8:2-3)

The way that God leads you may be through valleys deep.
The way that He leads you may climb a rocky steep.
The way that He leads you sometimes is sunny bright,
but sometimes He'll choose to lead you
through paths as dark as night.

As you yield to His leading, you'll find Him very near;
the comfort of His presence will calm your every fear.
You may think you've lost your bearing and despair of getting home,
but when Jesus Christ is leading
you will never walk alone. *

Sometimes we think of God's leading in our lives as primarily to guide us to a particular place. It is so much more. Sometimes it is to test us, to know what is in our heart, or to train us. Sometimes it is to teach us about the goodness of our Great Shepherd. Jesus said, *"I am the good shepherd; the good shepherd lays down His life for the sheep. . . . My sheep . . . follow Me; and I give eternal life to them . . . they shall never perish"* (John 10:11, 27-28).

May His goodness and faithfulness encourage you on your path today.

117

Break Thou the Bread of Life

Man does not live by bread alone, but man lives by every word that comes from the mouth of the Lord. (Deuteronomy 8:3 ESV)

A statement made by a visiting pastor startled and challenged our friend. Holding up his Bible, the pastor said, "Anyone who does not have an appetite for this Book, the Word of God, is either spiritually dead or spiritually very sick." That statement exposed our friend's personal "lack of appetite" and brought about life change in her heart.

In 1877, Mary Lathbury wrote verses expressing appetite for both the Bible and for Jesus, who said, *"I AM the bread of life"* (John 6:35 ESV).

Break now the bread of life, dear Lord, to me,
As You did break the loaves beside the sea;
Beyond the sacred page I seek You, Lord;
My spirit pants for You, O living Word.

Please bless the truth, dear Lord, to me, to me;
As You did bless the bread by Galilee;
Then shall all bondage cease, all fetters fall;
And I shall find my peace, my all in all.

You are the bread of life, O Lord, to me,
Your holy Word the truth that saves me;
Give me to eat and live with You above;
Teach me to love Your truth, for You are love.

O send Your Spirit, Lord, now unto me,
That He may touch my eyes, and make me see;
Show me the truth concealed within Your Word,
And in Your Book revealed I see the Lord.

118

New Creation

Therefore, if anyone is in Christ, he is a new creation; old things have passed away; behold all things have become new. (2 Corinthians 5:17)

"I knelt down a tramp and stood up a lady," is the testimony of Iris Urrey Blue as she looks back on the moment when, led by a young man who had been faithfully witnessing to her for months, she kneeled on the sidewalk in front of *The Inferno*, her Houston, Texas, topless bar. With countless abortions and heroin behind her, she has gone on to be one of God's beautiful trophies of grace, having miraculously been made over into a "New Creation" in Christ.

I have been made a New Creation,
with Christ, I have been crucified.
And what I was, I am no longer
because I died when Jesus died.

I have been made a New Creation,
though I was part of Adam's tree
I now am grafted into Jesus;
I am in Him, and He's in me.

I can't explain, it is a mystery,
I don't know how it can be true.
I just accept what He's accomplished,
I'm born again, all things are new. *

119

You Are My God

When You said, "Seek My face," My heart said to You, "Your face, Lord, I will seek." (Psalm 27:8 NKJV)

You are my God, I seek Your face,
You are my God, infinite grace.
You are my God, faithful and true,
You are my God, I worship You. +

The memory is very vivid. We were to be soloists that evening at a special concert, and I was not well. Added to that was the awareness that my recent attitude and reactions had not been Christ-like, and I felt like such a failure. I know I had read the passage before, but this time as I read Isaiah 41:9b-10, the Holy Spirit clearly spoke the words to my heart: *"You are my servant, I have chosen you and not rejected you. Do not fear, for I am with you. Do not anxiously look about you, for I am your God. I will strengthen you, surely I will help you . . ."*

He is MY God! Oh, what a difference it made at that moment to know that this is so! And what a difference it makes to have that confidence, whatever the circumstance may be. He wants His children to come with confidence into His presence. When we seek Him, He draws near to us and something wonderful happens in that intimate fellowship—we are being changed!

We all, with unveiled face beholding as in a mirror the glory of the Lord, are being transformed into the same image from glory to glory, just as from the Lord, the Spirit. (2 Corinthians 3:18 NKJV)

120

Here Is Love, Vast as the Ocean

Wales: 1904–1905 was a period that can only be explained by God being pleased to visit that principality of one million people in revival. It is estimated that in a period of six months, approximately one hundred thousand names were added to the Lamb's Book of Life. Subsequently, many chapels (church buildings) were built that, to this day, though no longer places where people gather to worship, have on their rock facades: 1904 or 1905.

A unique feature of the Welsh Revival was the importance of music in the meetings that sometimes lasted all night. During this time, one particular song surfaced that would become what was called the "love song of the revival," *Dyma gariad fel y moroedd.*

Here is love, vast as the ocean,
Loving kindness as the flood,
When the Prince of Life, our Ransom
Shed for us His precious blood.
Who would not His love remember?
Who can cease to sing His praise?
He can never be forgotten
Throughout Heaven's eternal days.

On the mount of crucifixion
Fountains opened deep and wide.
Through the floodgates of God's mercy
Flowed a vast and gracious tide.
Grace and love, like mighty rivers
Flowed unending from above.
God's own peace and perfect justice
Kissed my guilty world in love.

121

Let's Pray

There was no other way; the others had to go on to fulfill our ministry commitment. A back injury had occurred while dealing with heavy luggage in the rush to catch our overseas flight, and regardless of what position I tried, I could not find relief from the pain. Now alone and hurting in a foreign land, minutes seemed like hours. After a period of time, I "heard" it—a song that accompanied a gradual lessening and then complete cessation of the pain.

Someone's praying, Lord, kum ba yah!
Someone's praying, Lord, kum ba yah!
Someone's praying, Lord, kum ba yah!
O Lord, kum ba yah!

The song "replayed itself" many times in my mind. The Lord was listening and responding to one of His children who was interceding for me in prayer! God was demonstrating the fact that He gives His children the high privilege of coming before His throne to intercede for others.

The Apostle Paul shared with Corinthian believers what God had done for him and asked them to be involved in the days ahead: *". . . you also joining in helping us through your prayers, that thanks may be given by many persons on our behalf for the favor bestowed upon us through the prayers of many"* (2 Corinthians 1:11). God allows us to participate with Him through prayer in places and situations we can scarcely imagine. Let's pray!

122

Doxology

*For of him, and through him, and to him, are all things, to whom be glory
forever. Amen. (Romans 11:36 NKJV)*

May 22, 1954: It was the final day of the Greater London Crusade
and Billy Graham was exhausted. Though the weather was terrible, every
one of the one hundred thousand seats in Wembley Stadium was filled,
with an additional twenty-two thousand sitting on the playing field.

The Crusade meetings had lasted for three months, and Billy
didn't know where he was going to get the strength as he stood to preach
on "Choose You This Day Whom You Will Serve." But as he looked
over the crowd of one hundred twenty-two thousand wet, cold people,
God gave him the strength. That night, two thousand responded to the
invitation.

In all, more than thirty-eight thousand people made professions
of faith during that crusade. We have become acquainted over the years
with several men who were converted at that time who went on to become
pastors.

As the team bus made its way through the shouting, waving
crowds leaving the stadium, the whole Graham team began singing the
Doxology, which is the last verse of a fourteen-stanza hymn written by
Thomas Ken in 1695. Little could Ken have known the impact that those
four lines of poetry, translated into countless languages, would make on
the Christian world down through the centuries, even to our day.

Praise God from whom all blessings flow.
Praise Him all creatures here below.
Praise Him above ye heavenly hosts.
Praise Father, Son and Holy Ghost.

123

How Firm a Foundation

If the foundations are destroyed, what can the righteous do? (Psalm 11:3)

On September 11, 2001, America was shaken when two passenger jet planes were flown into New York City's Twin Towers and a separate plane was flown into the Pentagon in Washington D.C. Three thousand people died, and many others were injured.

Huddled under a hospital bed, as the Japanese bombed their city in 1941, Bertha Smith, former SBC missionary to China and Taiwan, sang the stanzas of the following hymn to her Chinese nursing students who were with her. Miss Bertha, as she was fondly known, knew where to look when the foundations seemed to be destroyed.

How firm a foundation, ye saints of the Lord
Is laid for your faith in His excellent Word!
What more can He say than to you He hath said,
To you who for refuge to Jesus have fled?

"Fear not, I am with thee; O be not dismayed,
For I am thy God, and will still give thee aid;
I'll strengthen thee, help thee, and cause thee to stand
Upheld by My righteous, omnipotent hand

The soul that on Jesus hath leaned for repose
I will not, I will not desert to his foes;
That soul, though all hell should endeavor to shake,
I'll never, no, never, no, never forsake!"

***

Thanks be to God, who gives us the victory through our Lord Jesus Christ.
(1 Corinthians 15:57)

141

124

O for a Thousand Tongues to Sing

Worthy is the Lamb that was slain to receive power and riches and wisdom and might and honor and glory and blessing. (Revelation 5:12)

On May 21, 1749, Charles Wesley wrote a hymn to celebrate the eleventh anniversary of his conversion. He titled it, "For the Anniversary of One's Conversion." We now know it as . . .

Oh, for a thousand tongues to sing
My great Redeemer's praise,
The glories of my God and king,
The triumphs of His grace!

My gracious Master and my God,
Assist me to proclaim,
To spread through all the earth abroad,
The honors of Thy name.

Jesus! the name that charms our fears,
That bids our sorrows cease—
'Tis music in the sinner's ears,
'Tis life, and health, and peace.

He breaks the pow'r of canceled sin,
He sets the pris'ner free;
His blood can make the foulest clean,
His blood availed for me.

125

Have You No Scar?

But He was wounded for our transgressions, He was bruised for our iniquities:
the chastisement of our peace was upon him; and with his stripes we are healed.
(Isaiah 53:5 KJV)

On December 16, 1867, in Millisle, County Down, Northern Ireland, a baby was born who was destined to become one of God's special servants. Her name? Amy Carmichael. Amy would spend most of her life ministering in India, founding the Dohnavur Fellowship, a home and school for rescued children, many of them young girls that had been offered by their parents as temple prostitutes. At Dohnavur, the children were educated and trained to serve God as Christian nurses, teachers, and evangelists.

In addition to her children's rescue ministry, she was a prolific writer and poet. Many of her poems speak to her own testing, being bedridden for the final twenty years of her life due to a near fatal fall that seriously injured her spine.

Have you no scar, no hidden scar in foot or side or hand?
I hear them say, "You're mighty in the land;"
And you may think yourself a rising star! Have you no scar?

Have you no wound? Yet I was wounded there on Calvary
With nails and spear for all the world to see.
But look, a million lives from death have bloomed.
Have you no wound?

No wound? No scar? Yet as the Master shall the servant be,
And bruised and torn the feet that follow Me;
But yours are whole, can he have followed far
Who has no wound? Who has no scar?

126

The Fullness of Time

In the fullness of time, God poured Himself into flesh and blood, visiting the earth as a man, walking among us—a King in disguise, the Creator among His creatures. While the Jews were waiting for a Messiah to triumphantly ride in on a white horse, who would deliver them from the tyranny of Rome, our Savior slipped down the back steps, to be born in a stable—and the world was forever changed.

In the fullness of time, God stooped down to the earth.
In the fullness of time, a miraculous birth.
In the fullness of time, when all things were in place,
In the fullness of time, man would look on God's face.

All the plans of the ages from eternity past,
in the womb of a virgin, culminated at last.
From the throne room of heaven to no room in the inn.
From the splendor of glory, to a world lost in sin,
in the fullness of time . . . *

When the fullness of the time had come, God sent forth His Son, born of a woman, born under the law, to redeem those who were under the law, that we might receive the adoption as sons. (Galatians 4:4-5 NKJV)

127

God's Ways Are Not Our Ways

As the heavens are higher than the earth, so are my ways higher than your ways and my thoughts than your thoughts. (Isaiah 55:9)

In lowly circumstances Jesus came,
and few there were who even knew His name.
A stable, sheep, a manger bed,
and on His mother's lap our Lord was fed,
God's ways are not our ways.

Can this be God, is this the Promised One?
Can this be He, God's one and only Son?
How can it be, so humble is His birth?
Why would God choose this way to come to earth?
God's ways are not our ways.

In lowly circumstances Jesus came.
He did not seek earth's fortunes, nor its fame.
And of this world's possessions nothing claimed;
to do God's will, for this alone He came—
God's ways are not our ways. *

How ashamed we would be if we could recognize how often our actions show that we are more concerned with ourselves than in seeking first the kingdom of God and His righteousness, as we read in Matthew 6:33. We can only repent as we reflect upon our Lord who, *"though He was in the form of God, did not count equality with God a thing to be grasped, but made himself nothing, taking the form of a servant . . ."* (Philippians 2:6-7).

Lord, may Your ways become my ways today, for Jesus' sake.

128

Saga of a Star

On a night of old three men, we're told,
made a trip bringing spices and gold.
They were wise, you see, perhaps with earned degrees
in Eastern astrology.
And they followed a light for a star was bright
and it led to where Jesus lay.
O praise God for that night and the heavenly light
that led to where Jesus lay.

To shepherds and sages, the mystery of ages
was revealed by the light of that star.
For the great God of glory, as angels tell the story,
left heaven to be where we are.
So I'll follow that light, for a star is still bright
and it leads to where Jesus lay.
O praise God for that night and the heavenly light
that leads to where Jesus lay.
O star of wonder, star of light. Star with radiant beauty, bright.

Oh, that star, oh, that star, it has shone for me,
shone in my night 'til my heart could see
that the child born that night came for Calvary,
came to die, shed His blood, came to set me free.

Let it sing, let is soar, let the music swell.
God come to earth, our Immanuel.
Lift your eyes to the skies, there His star appears,
Christ has come, hope is born, love has conquered, HE IS HERE. +

129

He Is Here!

Unto you is born this day . . . a Savior, who is Christ the Lord. You will find a baby . . . lying in a manger. (Luke 2:11-12 KJV)

Tiny hands, tiny hands of an infant,
reaching up in simplicity.
Unblemished, pure, trusting, and blameless
would one day be nailed to a tree.
Ordained in the throne room of heaven,
planned by God before time had begun;
Living Word, who brought order from chaos,
all the glory of heaven in One.

He is here, He is here, the Messiah.
It's the fullness of time, He has come.
Heaven's treasure, the brightest of jewels,
He is with us, the Savior, God's Son.

But, so many just pulled down the shutters,
they preferred not to know it was day.
They rebelled against God's intervention
and they chose to keep going their way.
But all those who were honest and open,
who were tired of a cloud-covered sun,
were invaded by God's light from heaven,
and they knew that Messiah had come.

Hallelujah, all glory to Jesus,
Hallelujah, all praise to His name.
Heaven's light invaded sin's darkness
the night the Savior came. *

130

A Land that Is Fairer than Day

Reverend Yona Kanamuzeyi was a Tutsi pastor in Rwanda, East Africa, who had established a network of twenty-four village churches that ministered to over six thousand people. In 1963, during the Hutu attempt to annihilate the hated Tutsi minority, he was arrested, along with thousands of others, and placed in a refugee camp.

On January 24, 1964, Pastor Kanamuzeyi, along with his friend, Andrew Kayumba, was put in a jeep and driven to a military camp. On the way, the pastor, knowing what was going to happen, said to his friend, "Let us surrender our lives into God's hand." Upon arrival at the military camp, he prayed in front of the soldiers, "Lord, avenge our innocent blood, and help these soldiers who do not know what they are doing."

Both men were tied up, and as pastor Kanamuzeyi was led toward a bridge over a river, he turned to ask Andrew one final question: "Do you believe, brother?" Andrew replied, "Yes, I believe." Andrew, who was subsequently released, told how, as his pastor was walking across the bridge, he heard him singing:

> *There's a land that is fairer than day,*
> *And by faith we can see it afar;*
> *For the Father waits over the way*
> *To prepare us a dwelling place there.*

That was as far as he got as the crack of gunshot silenced his voice—but not his life, for even as the soldiers were throwing his body into the river, the soul of pastor Kanamuzeyi was entering the presence of the One who was "waiting over the way," to welcome His faithful servant to the "land that is fairer than day."

131

No Home of His Own

He defined the role of an itinerate minister, his motto being, "Go into every kitchen and shop, address all on the salvation of their souls." He became one of America's early "circuit riders." He traveled over three hundred thousand miles on horseback for forty-five years. He had no home of his own but found shelter wherever he could.

When Francis Asbury arrived in America, there were three hundred Methodists and four Methodist ministers, all on the Atlantic seaboard. At the time of his death in 1816, Methodism had spread to every state, and more than 214,000 called themselves Methodists. Francis Asbury, himself, ordained more than four thousand ministers and preached more than sixteen thousand sermons.

His zeal for God and service began at his conversion at the age of seventeen. He immediately began preaching, and when he was but twenty-one, he heard John Wesley's call for ministers to go to America. Young Francis answered: "Here I am, send me."

America owes much to those early Methodists, and to Charles Wesley, whose hymns, such as the one below, formed the basis of congregational singing across the New World.

Oh, for a thousand tongues to sing my great Redeemer's praise,
The glories of my God and king, the triumphs of His grace!

My gracious Master and my God, assist me to proclaim,
To spread through all the earth abroad, the honors of Thy name.

Jesus! The name that charms our fears, that bids our sorrows cease—
'Tis music in the sinner's ears, 'tis life, and health, and peace.

He breaks the power of canceled sin, He sets the prisoner free;
His blood can make the foulest clean, His blood availed for me.

132

Yours, Not Mine

But he was wounded for our transgressions, He was bruised for our iniquities:
The chastisement of our peace was upon him; and with his stripes we are healed.
(Isaiah 53:5 ESV)

Your wounds, not mine, have healed my soul.
Your stripes, O Christ, have made me whole.
Your cross, not mine, has borne the load
of sin, and brought me to my God.

Your death, not mine, has paid the price,
the ransom due, the sacrifice.
Your righteousness has covered me;
Your blood, not mine, has set me free.

And so, I owe my all to You,
there's nothing else that I can do
but lift my eyes again to see
the Christ, the Lamb of Calvary. *

Prayer

Gracious Holy Spirit, make this precious truth fresh and real to my heart
again. With a glad and free spirit, let me serve and follow Jesus, the One who
purchased me with His own shed blood.

133

To My World He Came

[God has] spoken to us by His Son, whom He has appointed heir of all things, through whom also He made the worlds. (Hebrews 1:2b NKJV)

From Heaven's matchless glory to this earth and sin's domain.
Through history's brightest hour to its cruelest, deepest pain.
From God's throne room to a manger, then a wooden cross of shame.
It was to this kind of world the Savior came.

From eternity to man's present day;
from those golden streets to earth's dusty way;
from the throne room of heaven to a manger of hay,
to my world the Savior came.

From the council-room of heaven to the shame of Pilate's Hall.
"Crucify Him! Crucify Him!" were the words He'd hear them call.
From the grapes of heaven's vineyards to man's vinegar and gall,
it was to this kind of world the Savior came.

From a life that knew no time and space,
to a lost and dying human race,
from the presence of His Father's face,
to my world, the Savior came. *

It is an awesome truth—our Lord Jesus chose to truly identify Himself with us. He lived in a human body like ours. *"He had to be made like his brothers in every respect, so that He might become a merciful and faithful high priest in the service of God, to make propitiation for the sins of the people."* And *"because He himself has suffered when tempted, He is able to help those who are being tempted"* (Hebrews 2:17-18 ESV).

Prayer

Thank you, Lord, for being willing to step into my world!

134

Our God Is Worthy of Praise

Sing to the Lord, bless his name; tell of his salvation from day to day ... great is the Lord, and greatly to be praised. (Psalm 96:2-4)

Our God is worthy of praise, Lord of Lords, the Ancient of Days.
His power is glorious, He reigns victorious,
His truth and mercy will never end.
Our God is worthy of praise!

I praise You, Lord! I praise You, Lord!
I bless and praise You for Who You are!
You made the land and You made the sea,
and, O my God, You also made me!

I praise Your name! I praise Your name,
Exalted in splendor and mighty to save!
You made the land and You made the sea,
and, O my God, You also made me.
MY GOD IS WORTHY OF PRAISE! [+]

Just think. God made me! God made you! This great God who created planets, seas, mountains, the sun, the moon, and the stars also deliberately created you and created me. As the psalmist expressed to God, *"You formed my inward parts; You knitted me together in my mother's womb. I praise You, for I am fearfully and wonderfully made"* (Psalm 139:13-14). Jesus told the disciples, *"Even the hairs of your head are all numbered"* (Matthew 10:30). He said, *"As the Father has loved me, so have I loved you"* (John 15:9). God made us, loves us, and gives our lives meaning. *"We are his workmanship, created in Christ Jesus for good works, which God prepared beforehand, that we should walk in them"* (Ephesians 2:10). Our God IS worthy of praise!

135

Songs of Praise

Praise the Lord! Praise him for his mighty deeds; praise him according to his excellent greatness. . . . Let everything that has breath praise the Lord!
(Psalm 150:1-2, 6)

Songs of praise the angels sang,
heaven with hallelujahs rang,
when creation was begun,
when God spoke, and it was done.
Songs of praise awoke the morn
when the Prince of Peace was born.
Songs of praise arose when He
left the tomb in victory.

Heaven and earth will pass away;
songs of praise will crown that day.
God will make new heaven and earth,
songs of praise shall hail that birth.
And until His kingdom comes,
and His work on earth is done,
we, the church, are called to raise
psalms and hymns and songs of praise.

Saints below with heart and voice
with their songs of praise, rejoice.
Learning now, through faith and love,
songs that we will sing above.
When we breathe that final breath,
songs of praise shall drown out death.
When to'rd heaven our spirits fly,
SONGS OF PRAISE SHALL FILL THE SKY! *

136

Our Refuge and Our Strength

God is our refuge and our strength, a very present help in trouble. Therefore we will not fear, though the earth be removed, and though the mountains be carried into the sea. . . . There is a river whose streams make glad the City of our God.
(Psalm 46:1-2, 4 NKJV)

God is our refuge and our strength,
a tested help in times of trouble.
And so, we need not ever fear;
if the earth should change or the mountains crumble,
God always is our refuge and our strength.

Come see the glorious things God does,
that He's in charge is very clear.
The wars man makes, He'll bring to end
by breaking bow and cutting spear—
stand silent! Know that He, the Lord is God.

There is a river whose streams make glad the City of our God.
The holy dwelling place of the Most High.
God is right there in the midst of her and she will not be moved.
The Lord of Hosts is with us, He is nigh.

STAND SILENT! KNOW THAT HE, THE LORD, IS GOD *

137

Nothing that I have Done

For by grace you have been saved through faith; and that not of yourselves,
it is the gift of God; not as a result of works, that no one should boast.
(Ephesians 2:8-9)

No works these hands have done
can save my guilty soul.
No striving that my flesh has tried
can make my spirit whole.
All that I feel or do
can't give me peace with God.
Not all my prayers, my hopes, my tears
can bear sin's heavy load.

Your grace, alone, O Lord
can pardon me from sin.
Your power, alone, O Son of God
can cleanse me deep within.
I bless You, praise You, Lord,
I rest on love divine,
and with these faltering lips and heart
I call You, Savior—MINE! *

We could never earn this grace that God has provided to us. We could never be "good enough" to deserve it. But we can gratefully receive it and recognize that this gift is possible because of our Savior, the Lord Jesus.

138

A Morning Prayer

O Lord, in the morning you hear my voice... (Psalm 5:3 ESV)

So much I need Your power today,
so much I need Your guiding hand.
So easily I lose my way,
so quickly fail to understand
that in my strength, all living is in vain.

It seems so quickly I forget
what You have done in days gone by,
when far from You I wandered, yet
in patient love You heard my cry
and brought me back to fellowship again.

So quietly I come today
to ask for guidance on the way.
That in my living, I'll not stray
from off Your path, these things I pray:
Your will, not mine, help me today. *

In His Sermon on the Mount, the Lord Jesus said, *"Blessed are the poor in spirit, for theirs is the kingdom of heaven"* (Matthew 5:3 ESV). Who are those who are poor in spirit? They are the ones who are aware of their total inadequacy apart from God—of their desperate need of His presence and guidance every day. Lord, hear this, my prayer.

139

Eternity's Goal in View

You do not know what your life will be like tomorrow. You are just a vapor that appears for a little while . . . (James 4:14)

Life's only a vapor, so quickly it's gone,
the next moment may never come.
My yesterdays never will, never return,
what's done in the past is done.

But I have this moment, this moment to live,
a moment that is brand new.
And live it I shall to the glory of God,
with eternity's goal in view.

Forgetting the things that now are behind,
and pressing straight on to'rd the goal,
with all of my body, my soul, and my mind,
with eternity's goal in view.

Not wasting my time on the things that are past,
the things that I can't undo,
but giving this day to what's going to last,
with eternity's goal in view. *

Today, whatever the past may be, today we can adopt the attitude of the Apostle Paul, who said, *"Forgetting what lies behind and reaching forward to what lies ahead, I press on toward the goal for the prize of the upward call of God in Christ Jesus"* (Philippians 3:13-14). Today, by God's grace, we can indeed live with eternity's goal in view.

140

Security

He will cover you with his pinions, and under his wings you will find refuge; his faithfulness is a shield and buckler. (Psalm 91:4)

How precious is your constant love, O God, Almighty King.
Humanity takes refuge in the shadow of your wing.
You nourish them on tables spread with food to feed their souls,
And let them drink from springs of life until their hearts
    o'erflow.

You are the Fountain of our life, the Light that lights our way.
The Fiery Pillar in the night, the Cloud that leads by day.
Unbounding Love, unfailing Friend, no earthly power can change,
And solid as the Rock on which we build, your truth remains.

Secure I am, whatever comes, as on the Rock I stand.
There is no safer place to be; all else is sinking sand.
Though storms may rage, the lightening flash,
and I may frightened be,
I am protected by the blood that flows from Calvary. *

My hope is built on nothing less
Than Jesus' blood and righteousness.
I dare not trust the sweetest frame,
But wholly lean on Jesus' name.

On Christ the solid rock I stand,
All other ground is sinking sand!

141

Jesus Loves Me

After the death of their father, Anna Warner and her sister Susan supported themselves with various literary endeavors. "Jesus Loves Me" was written to be included in one of the sister's novels. In the story, it was a poem that was read to a dying child.

Jesus loves me! This I know, for the Bible tells me so.
Little ones to Him belong; They are weak, but He is strong.

Jesus loves me! This I know, as He loved so long ago,
Taking children on His knee, saying, "Let them come to Me."

Jesus loves me! He who died Heaven's gate to open wide;
He will wash away my sin, Let His little child come in.

Yes, Jesus loves me! Yes, Jesus loves me!
Yes, Jesus loves me, the Bible tells me so.

The Bible gives us a beautiful picture of Jesus' response to little children. *"They were bringing children to him that he might touch them, and the disciples rebuked them. But when Jesus saw it, he was indignant and said to them, 'Let the children come to me; do not hinder them for to such belong the kingdom of God.' And he took them in his arms and blessed them"* (Mark 10:13-16).

What an encouragement this is, to know that even today we can bring the little ones in our lives to Him, as we call out their names to Him in prayer.

142

Crucified with Christ

I am crucified with Christ: nevertheless I live; yet not I, but Christ lives in me: and the life which I now live in the flesh I live by the faith of the Son of God, who loved me, and gave himself for me. (Galatians 2:20 KJV)

I've been crucified with Christ,
I was there when Jesus died.
I've been crucified with Christ,
to my life the blood's applied.
I've been crucified with Christ,
I am dead and yet alive.
Hallelujah, I've been crucified with Christ.

I've been crucified with Christ,
it's a fact of history.
I've been crucified with Christ,
yet it's still a mystery.
I've been crucified with Christ,
now my Savior lives in me.
Hallelujah, I've been crucified with Christ.

I've been crucified with Christ,
I will never be the same.
I've been crucified with Christ,
since I'm dead I can't complain.
I've been crucified with Christ,
yet I live through Jesus' name.
HALLELUJAH, I'VE BEEN CRUCIFIED WITH CHRIST. *

143

He the Pearly Gates Will Open

The twelve gates were twelve pearls: each individual gate was of one pearl. And the street of the city was pure gold, like transparent glass. (Revelation 21:21 NKJV)

Love divine, so great and wondrous, deep and mighty, pure, sublime!
Coming from the heart of Jesus, just the same through tests of time.
He the pearly gates will open,
so that I may enter in;
For He purchased my redemption
and forgave me all my sin.

Like a dove when hunted, frightened, as a wounded fawn was I;
Brokenhearted, yet He healed me, He will heed the sinner's cry.
Love divine, so great and wondrous,
all my sins He then forgave!
I will sing His praise forever,
For His blood, His power to save.

In life's eventide, at twilight, at His door I'll knock and wait;
By the precious love of Jesus I shall enter Heaven's gate.
He the pearly gates will open,
so that I may enter in;
For He purchased my redemption
and forgave me all my sin.

144

Condemned

As in Adam all die, so also in Christ shall all be made alive. (1 Corinthians 15:22)

In prison darkness I had lived so long.
I could not sing because I had no song.
I knew the reason why I was condemned;
I'd made my last appeal—this was the end.

Behind sin's bars death's shadow crossed my face;
I sat there, part of Adam's fallen race
when down the corridor I heard a voice:
"A second Adam's here! You've got a choice!
A choice to die yourself, or let him be
the One to die for you, while you go free."

A second Adam? What was that to me?
How could a second Adam set me free?
Then suddenly a light shone in that cell—
I realized what I deserved was hell,
and now, a God of love had seen my plight
and sent His Son to take my place that night.

The sun was darkened as my Savior died,
when on the cross my Lord was crucified.
No earthly judge would set this prisoner free,
then Jesus came to die in place of me.
All by Himself upon that cross of shame
outside the city wall the Lamb was slain.
The pure, the spotless Lamb of God was He.
How can it be? He died to set me free. *

145

Lord, Do It Again

Restore us again, O God; make your face shine upon us that we might be saved.
(Psalm 80:3 NIV)

The year was 1865. The place? The Dutch Reformed Church on Fulten Street, New York City. The man? Jeremiah Lanphier. The event? Wednesday, noon hour prayer meetings. First week—six attended. Second week—twenty. It soon became a daily event and continued to grow and spread until other venues, including police stations and firehouses, had to be added all across the city.

The *New York Times* sent reporters daily to report on the numbers. It began to spread up the east coast then across the nation. Coast to coast, prayer meetings were being held. Within a year it was estimated that over one million converts were added to the churches of America. Lord, do it again. Pour out Your Spirit upon us!

> Lord, how we long to see You work in power,
> we need revival in our land today.
> You have encouraged us with every shower,
> but Lord, it's for a mighty rain we pray.
>
> You've let us hear the rustling in the bushes.
> We've seen a cloud the size of a man's hand.
> We've read what You have done down through the ages,
> O Lord, we need revival in our land.
>
> Lord, not for praise of man, but for Your glory.
> Lord, not that we might boast, but for Your name.
> Forgive us, cleanse us, fill us with Your Spirit,
> O Lord, revive Your people once again. *

146

Just as I Am

In her thirties, Charlotte Elliott experienced a serious illness that left her in poor health and pain for the rest of her life. As a result of this, she battled severe depression for years.

One day, when Charlotte was especially depressed, Dr. Caesar Malan, a Swiss pastor, musician, and close friend, visited the Elliott family. He felt led to ask her whether she had ever experienced God's peace in the midst of her difficulties. This upset Charlotte, but later, she confided in Dr. Malan that she wanted to come to Jesus but didn't know how, to which he simply replied, "Come to Him just as you are." Some time later, during a bout of depression, she recalled his words and began to write her response to what Dr. Malan had said:

Just as I am, without one plea, but that Thy blood was shed for me,
And that Thou bidst me come to Thee, O Lamb of God, I come

Just as I am, and waiting not to rid my soul of one dark blot,
To Thee whose blood can cleanse each spot, O Lamb of God, I come

Just as I am, though tossed about with many a conflict, many a doubt,
Fightings and fears within, without, O Lamb of God, I come,

Just as I am, poor, wretched, blind; sight, riches, healing of the mind,
Yea, all I need in Thee to find, O Lamb of God, I come.

Over a century later, when young Billy Graham went forward to receive Christ, they were singing "Just as I Am," an invitation he would eventually use throughout his evangelistic ministry.

147

Child of My Child
(The Grandparent Song)

Let the little children to come to me, and do not forbid them, for of such is the kingdom of heaven. (Matthew 19:14 NKJV)

Child of my child, I love you, you are a part of me.
By the miracle of creation, you're the child of my child, you see.
One day you'll know what I'm saying,
one day you'll understand
when you have a child of your child
to hold like I'm holding your hand.

Child of my child, God loves you, I know this really is true.
When Jesus lived here among us, He called children just like you.
He called boys and girls to come near Him,
He told them about God's great love.
He said if they'd trust and believe Him,
He'd prepare them a place up above.

A place that will be bright like diamonds,
a place that will have streets of gold.
A place where there'll be no more crying,
a place where nobody gets old.
A place where we'll live on forever,
a place where it never will rain.
A place where God's Son is the sunshine,
a place where there'll be no more pain. *

148

Footprints of Jesus

Never will I leave you; never will I forsake you. (Hebrews 13:5 NIV)

I dreamed that I was looking back from heaven
upon the journey I had made from birth.
I dreamed that I was standing there with Jesus,
discussing what had happened down on earth.
He pointed out where we had walked together,
and I could see His footprints next to mine.
They started where I trusted Him as Savior,
two sets of footprints in the sands of time.

But then I saw something that was a mystery,
those places where it seemed I walked alone.
Those times when there was just one set of footprints;
I asked Him where it was that He had gone.
He looked at me and said: "I didn't leave you.
The set of footprints that you see are mine.
Those were the times, my child, when you were carried,
those are my footprints in the sands of time."

When life gets hard, and nights are long,
He carries me, He gives a song.
I am secure, I fear no harm
when I am held in Jesus' arms.
One set of footprints, sometimes two,
when there's just one, He's carrying you.
He'll carry you, He'll hold your hand.
FOOTPRINTS OF JESUS in the sand. *

149

Prayer for Our Nation

Righteousness exalts a nation, but sin is a disgrace to any people.
(Proverbs 14:34)

O Father, heal our nation,
Lord, would You stay Your hand?
In wrath, remember mercy,
please Lord, please heal our land.
We know we've deeply grieved You,
we've sinned and brought You shame,
O Father God, forgive us, we pray in Jesus' name.

Our nation, Lord, is crumbling, it's crumbling from within.
And we have watched it happen, O God, forgive our sin.
The wound is deep and bleeding, and BAND-AIDs® will not do,
O God for major surgery we turn our hearts to You.

Lord, we've replaced Your glory with man-made pageantry.
We've sung, we've danced, we've strutted for all the world to see.
But Lord, where is the power, the power that conquers sin?
O Lord, we humbly ask You, "Revive your church again."

You said if we would humble ourselves and seek Your face,
You said if we would pray "Lord" and turn from sin's disgrace
that You would hear from heaven, that You would stay Your hand.
O Lord, we cry for mercy—O God, please heal our land. *

150

God Will Take Care of You

... casting all your anxiety on Him, because He cares for you. (1 Peter 5:7)

Pastor Stillman Martin had been asked to preach several hours from his home when his wife suddenly became ill. He was about to cancel the engagement when his youngest son spoke up: "Father, don't you think that God wants you to preach today? He will take care of mother." Pastor Martin made the trip, and while he was gone, his wife, Civilla, wrote the following hymn-poem.

Be not dismayed whate'er betide. God will take care of you;
Beneath his wings of love abide,
God will take care of you;

Through days of toil when heart doth fail, God will take care of you;
When dangers fierce your path assail,
God will take care of you.

All you may need he will provide, God will take care of you;
Trust him and you will be satisfied,
God will take care of you.

No matter what may be the test, God will take care of you;
Lean, weary one, upon his breast,
God will take care of you.

God will take care of you; through every day, o'er all the way;
He will take care of you,
GOD WILL TAKE CARE OF YOU.

Notes